BEHAVIOR ANALYTICS
IN RETAIL

BEHAVIOR ANALYTICS IN RETAIL

MEASURE, MONITOR AND PREDICT EMPLOYEE AND CUSTOMER
ACTIVITIES TO OPTIMIZE STORE OPERATIONS AND PROFITABILITY,
AND ENHANCE THE SHOPPING EXPERIENCE

Ronny Max

authorHOUSE®

AuthorHouse™ LLC
1663 Liberty Drive
Bloomington, IN 47403
www.authorhouse.com
Phone: 1-800-839-8640

Published by AuthorHouse   09/24/2013

ISBN: 978-1-4918-0627-2 (sc)
ISBN: 978-1-4918-0630-2 (e)

Library of Congress Control Number: 2013914272

Any people depicted in stock imagery provided by Thinkstock are models, and such images are being used for illustrative purposes only.
Certain stock imagery © Thinkstock.

This book is printed on acid-free paper.

Because of the dynamic nature of the Internet, any web addresses or links contained in this book may have changed since publication and may no longer be valid. The views expressed in this work are solely those of the author and do not necessarily reflect the views of the publisher, and the publisher hereby disclaims any responsibility for them.

CONTENTS

WHY MEASURE BEHAVIOR

What is the value of a bricks-and-mortar store? As retailers move to a multi-channel world where the winners must overcome the challenges of pricing transparency, personalized marketing, and supply chain controls, most sales still happen in the physical site. Behavior Analytics is the science of studying the behavior of people. Schedule to Demand is a subset of Behavior Analytics, a method that correlates between traffic, sales and labor data, in order to optimize the productivity of employees and position them where they matter most.

In Behavior Analytics for Retail, we will introduce the core metrics of Schedule to Demand; design the requirements for a Customer Service Model of the store, inside the store, and at the checkout; present technology options and accuracy requirements; and offer insights through case studies. Regardless of how the future would shape retail, the physical store will continue to exist, and thrive. We propose a framework for retailers, and others, on how to optimize store operations and profitability, and enhance the shopping experience by measuring, monitoring and predicting the behavior of employees and customers.

Analytics in retail is primarily used in marketing, merchandising, and, of course, ecommerce, but we will focus on the physical store. Retailers have three core costs in the store—real-estate, inventory, and labor. Traffic monitoring adds value by measuring the sales conversion, improving layouts, and marketing effectiveness. We address each of these metrics, but our focus is workforce optimization and its impact on the shopping experience.

Buying behavior refers to what the customer purchases, and we received that data from the point-of-sale system. The shopping behavior starts with the intent to buy and ends when the customer buys, or not. We will deal with the shopping behavior in a bricks-and-mortar store.

By the time a customer enters the store, the only variables are the employees. The manager cannot control layout and inventory. The store manager cannot change branding, promotions, and much of the in-store marketing. In most cases, the standard schedule is mandated by corporate. The small piece of control by the store manager is management in real-time, where to position the employees, and the priority of their tasks.

Unfortunately, since service is not measured definitively, it is usually the last task on the list. Schedule to Demand aims to change this framework by allowing retailers to design, monitor and predict service metrics in a Customer Service Model.

Measuring behaviors started with people counting technologies at the door. In the 1980s, retailers placed infrared beams at the entrance to count how many customers are entering and exiting the store in order to calculate sales conversion. The idea was simple—divide transactions by arrivals and calculate the conversion rate from browsers to buyers. After stumbling around for decades, humbled by inaccurate counts, the glory of point-of-sale data, and the burden of allocating scarce capital resources, door-counting technologies and the business benefits from measuring the sales conversion entered mainstream retail.

Once retailers had demand trends and sales conversion data, the obvious question was—how do we increase the conversion rate? This is the origin of Schedule to Demand.

Customer Service Models define the metrics for all phases of the sales cycle, from entry, to browsing to checkout, and building a policy of customer service. Key Performance Indicators include the Sales Opportunities, Sales Conversion, Service Intensity, Service Productivity, Browsing Behaviors, Queue Management and Predictive Scheduling.

Optimization is about satisfying most customers, and not necessarily all anomalies, therefore we will also address the concept of success rates and advise caution when due. The intent is to prevent silos of information, and to encourage consistent, data-based communication methods that adhere to corporate policy while adapting to the local conditions in the store. Most importantly, we offer actionable metrics.

People Counting technology, such as video, thermal and wireless, is the core of Schedule to Demand. The technology serves three functions —capture objects, analyze behaviors, present information—including reporting and real-time applications. In addition to current technologies and solutions, we will discuss the requirements for accuracy and the proof-of-concept process.

Each retail category has its own tweaks, and we will present scenarios from the field. For specialty retailers, sales conversion and linear queues dominate. A luxury retailer may decide 30 minutes is an effective service time, while the company selling apparel to teenagers may say a ratio of 1 associate to 7 customers is sufficient. Supermarkets benefit from queue management at the frontline checkouts with the strategy of "One in Front". Big Box stores may desire a "No Queue" policy. Retail Banking and Quick Service Restaurants face similar challenges in their dense, destination stores, with customer service inside the store, servicing the drive-thru, and performing back-of-store activities, all competing for limited labor resources. Airports confront crowds huddled in long "snake" type queues. And Zone Monitoring integrates traffic behavior into innovative applications.

Retail is an industry where creativity and operational excellence is a winning combination, yet one cannot succeed without the other. This book mixes high-concept strategies and minute details, yet I keep, or at least try to maintain, the metrics and samples simple. Each chapter can be read by itself, but the themes of theory, technology, and tales are continuous.

Schedule to Demand is so new that I will risk the wrath of my colleagues by shamelessly defining terminology and designing theories. I have worked with many retailers and technology companies, but much of what is described here is still a preview of small-scale pilots and a few innovative retail executives. In that sense, this book is not a scientific review but a wish list.

If data is an objective measurement, information is data-in-context, and knowledge is the skill and ability to translate information into action, then Behavior Analytics, and our Schedule-to-Demand, is an attempt to sort the chaos out of traffic, sales and workforce data, into feasible metrics. I hope that together, we will journey into a profitable, and productive, experience in the store.

BOOK 1
Schedule to Demand

CHAPTER 1
CUSTOMER SERVICE MODEL

Schedule to Demand is the theory of optimizing store operations and profitability by measuring the customers and staff activities, and positioning employees where they matter most. The metrics and Key Performance Indicators (KPIs), designing a corporate service policy, and the adaptation to local conditions are defined in the Customer Service Model.

Customer Service Models are dynamic in the sense that their framework depends on the availability of information, continuous feedback, and the capability of the company to work with data. Models, by definition, are diagrams of how the retailer perceives the interaction with a customer, based on business objectives, and translated into measurable, and actionable, metrics.

We should begin the proof-of-concept process with designing the Customer Service Model, before any technology is vetted, but since Schedule to Demand is a dynamic method and the techniques are flexible, retailers can always stop, assess, and then move forward. Creating a frame of questions and feasible goals is not as simple as it sounds and it requires some soul searching by the organization. How retailers view, develop, and adapt customers service models varies by a market category, their history with counting technologies, and most important, their analytics culture.

This chapter introduces the basics of the Customer Service Model.

CUSTOMER SERVICE MODELS

In Behavior Analytics, the customer experience in the physical store has three core phases—entry, browsing and checkout. Measuring how many customers entered the store, per period of time, offers a framework for the store. Monitoring browsing activities allows for a real-time view of customers and staff activities. Based on the understanding of actual demand and past behaviors, we can predict the requirements for the checkout process, or the "last touch point". While each phase has its own Key Performance Indicators (KPIs), together they constitute the Customer Service Model.

The Bricks-and-Mortar Store

When customers step into a bricks-and-mortar store, they become a sales opportunity. The combination of traffic and point-of-sales data provides the sales conversion metrics, which is an objective by itself to many retailers. The reason is simple. Even a 1% increase in conversion has an exponential effect on sales, translating to millions of dollars for a chain of stores. As a result, many counting projects start with the goal of increasing the conversion from, say, 35% to 37% within 2 years. Once the traffic counters are installed, the sales conversion rate tends to dominate corporate policies, including compensation plans for store managers.

While sales conversion is by far the most accepted and known traffic metric in retail, it is not the only useful metric from door-counting. Marketing metrics are also a feature of measuring demand. Since Marketing is the department responsible for bringing customers to the stores, we can identify the effectiveness of promotions and campaigns by measuring changes in traffic, by location, and per period of time. While the correlation between traffic and promotion is not always direct and clear-cut, the information can provide insights on the value of marketing.

Schedule to Demand is exactly as it sounds. It originates from the links between demand and scheduling. Instead of the prevalent method of scheduling to transactions, the schedule takes into account not only buyers, but all the people who walked into the store. The move towards a demand-based process hinges on two metrics, Service Intensity and its Average Time Service as a frame for the store. Service Productivity becomes a benchmark for employees. While these service metrics are calculated from traffic to the store as a complete entity, their applications relate to behaviors inside the store.

The Shopping Experience

Analytics plays a crucial role in retail, including management of the supply chain and marketing, but how customers move and interact inside the store is a field limited in scope. At this point, retailers rely mostly on mystery shoppers, customer surveys, and point-of-sale data to glimpse information on browsing behaviors. While technology companies are actively researching and developing new ideas, we do not have traffic solutions for the full store that are both accurate and sensibly priced.

That said, we have ways to measure and monitor in real-time in order to improve the deployment of employees inside the store and adapt to actual demand. In-store behavior analytics is also the most promising nascent market once vendors can build applications that combine the traffic, marketing, inventory, and loss prevention systems.

The Last Touch Point

Customer Service Models for the checkout phase are the most talked, and misunderstood, facets of Schedule to Demand. The best known service model is the Frontline Service Management in supermarkets named "One in Front". Also known as "1+1", the queue solution measures, in real-time, how many customers are waiting in line, and predicts how many cashiers, or stations, should be open in order to have a only one customer waiting in the queue. Therefore, the customer service policy of "One in Front" says that in any given time, one customer is being served, and one customer waits in line. Currently, there are four large deployments in the world. Queue Management and Predictive Scheduling are emerging solutions.

In addition to supermarkets, queue management generates interest with Big Box and Department stores, Retail Banking, Quick Service Restaurants, and Airports. This led to a diverse array of queue models, including Five-Five for a maximum five customers waiting no longer than five minutes, Queue Flow to measure the exit speed from the queue, and the infamous No Queue.

"No Queue" is the most hyped, and most misinterpreted, model for customer service. Looking closer, there are really two kinds of "No Queue" models. The first is preventing the formation of queues at the checkout counter. The second is not having checkout counters. Both are based on using mobile devices, but the first relates to speeding the Transaction Time and Over-Staffing in frontline hubs and counters, while the second deals with a different concept of service, where the associate serves the customer throughout the sales cycle.

To understand why measuring demand is the key to scheduling optimization, we should explore the limitations of scheduling only with data from the point-of-sale.

THE SELF-FULFILLING PROPHECY OF TRANSACTIONS

The most common method to design the schedule is to use point-of-sale data. In Figure 1-1, we offer the following tale of two stores, which demonstrates how retailers can trap themselves in the less than desired state of missed sales opportunities.

Figure 1-1 Hello and Goodbye stores comparison

	Hello	Goodbye
Daily Visitors	1044	1035
Transactions	361	276
Sales Conversion	35%	27%
Payroll Hours	120	90
Service Intensity	9	12
Average Basket	$70	$60
Sales	$25,160	$16,560

Hello and Goodbye stores belong to the Special Chain, selling apparel and accessories. Both serve similar markets. Both are located in open air malls. Both serve the same demographics, located within a 20 minute drive from each other. If we only had point-of-sale data the results are evident—with $25,160, Hello has almost double the daily sales of the Goodbye store at $16,560.

If we only had the point-of-sale data, Hello is better than Goodbye in the other aspects. The average basket size in the Hello Store is higher than Goodbye, and Hello also has more transactions. For the corporate office, the relative success of Hello compared to Goodbye has direct implications on the functions of inventory, scheduling, and compensation.

Once we add demand data, it is obvious that the stores have the same sales potential. Assuming the stores have similar demographics, geography and layout characteristics, the level of traffic indicates the stores should perform on the same level.

The data provides some clues. First, the sales conversion in Goodbye is significantly lower than in Hello, with 27% to 35% respectively. This means Goodbye does not convert as many visitors to buyers as it should. This may be because the corporate office of Special Chain does not allocate as many desired items to Goodbye as it does to Hello, therefore cementing the less-performing status. The more interesting, and easy to fix, information is the payroll hours allocated to each store, with 120 hours allocated to Hello, and only 90 staff hours for Goodbye. From afar, corporate workforce system designed the schedule based on sales performance and as a result the Goodbye store was not staffed to service the actual demand.

The more service oriented the retailer; the more important it is to schedule correctly. For Special Stores, the lower ratio of Visitors to Associates (simplified Service Intensity) in Hello compared to Goodbye may have been the main cause why the store doubled sales. The story of Goodbye may be fictional, but almost every project of door-counting has these scenarios. A senior executive once summarized such a store with "we did this to ourselves".

KEY PERFORMANCE INDICATORS (KPIs)

Schedule to Demand is about translating the behaviors into metrics that are measured, monitored and predictable. The data allows us to manage, to understand the connections between sales, demand and workforce decisions. We do this with the Key Performance Indicators catered to each phase of the shopping experience; in other words, the metrics of the Customer Service Model.

In retail, the most important Key Performance Indicator is Comparable Sales (Comp Sales), which compares sales period-to-period for the same stores. While sales are the outcome of a successful strategy and execution, it does not describe the factors that influence sales.

Schedule to Demand is based on the following core metrics, which help retailers to increase sales.

Sales Opportunities

Traffic is another word for demand. The metric measures how many people entered the store, per period of time. In other words, each visitor to the store represents a sales opportunity.

If we measure the validity of a website we start with site visits, unique visitors, page views and only then the buyer conversion rate. If we work on a call center analysis we start with the number of calls and cost per call. Measuring and monitoring demand trends is the first step to increasing sales per store, and across the chain.

Demand can be measured by the number of people entering, people exiting, or occupancy, each is more appropriate according to the metric's objectives.

In general, we can categorize demand in three levels:

- **Low Volume Stores**: These stores tend to provide quality, and personalized, customer service. These stores have less than 200 visitors per day, and many customers are frequent shoppers.
- **High Volume Stores**: On the other side of the spectrum are big sized stores with more than 1,000 daily arrivals. Many of these stores are household names and serve as anchor stores in shopping malls. Some are destination stores. Some are subjected to the pressures of converting visitors to buyers.
- **Mid Volume Stores:** Many stores carry 200 to 1,000 daily visitors. From a service point of view, these stores face the challenge of providing one-on-one customer service without scheduling or training their sales associates appropriately. This is where Schedule to Demand originated.

Demand metrics such as traffic trends, customer value, and marketing productivity provide a more complete picture of the store's sales opportunity.

Sales Conversion

Sales Conversion measures how many browsers were converted to buyers, per period of time, and is the Key Performance Indicator for store operations. A common facet of behaviors for the retail store is the inverse correlation between Traffic and Sales Conversion. In other words, when traffic increases, sales conversion tends to go down. The tenet of Schedule to Demand is to supply tools so the store will operated at the same level of service, *regardless* of demand.

Sales Conversion is also commonly used in comparing a store's performance. If my experience is any guide, there are variations within a retail chain, and among direct competitors, to render general ratios as useless. Therefore, my rule of thumb is to compare a store's performance first against itself, second against peers with similar characteristics, and only then against the chain.

That said, we can see some general trends based on the customer's intent to buy.

- **Luxury Stores**: The low-traffic stores that sell discretionary income items, such as electronics or jewelry, have 3 to 15% sales conversion rates.
- **Specialty Stores:** Stores offering a specific niche, such as apparel or shoes, have a conversion rate from 20 to 50%. For these retailers, the shopping experience is defined by browsing behaviors.
- **Big Box Stores:** The line between pure destination stores and those that are not, is not always clear and is mostly attributed to location.

However, we can see the difference in behaviors and these stores typically experience a conversion rate of 65 to 85%.

- **Destination Stores:** Supermarkets and Big Box specialty stores tend to have conversion rates of 85% and higher. Simply put, a visitor is typically a buyer. In destination stores our focus should be on traffic anomalies such as abandon and group behaviors.

Instead of searching for a magic number, retailers should focus on improving the conversion rate of each store and across the chain.

Service Intensity

If Sales Conversion measures store performance than Service Intensity serves as the guide of how to optimize store operations. While the location and layout cannot be changed easily, inventory depends on supply chain control, and traffic relies on marketing investments, adapting the regular schedule to demand is a relatively quick fix. Most schedules are done two to four weeks ahead, and for many retailers the high turnover of their employees is a factor of doing business. This provides challenges and opportunities to quickly influence the shopping experience and hence increase sales.

Service Intensity can be calculated in a variety of ways, which directly impacts values. However, the limited data from the field suggests that the optimal ratio for the 15 minutes of schedule segments, the ratio of Visitors to Sales Associates, is from 4 to 9.

In addition, Service Intensity provides information on the Average Service Time, and the quality of sales associates with the Weighted Service Intensity. We also introduce Service Level Measurement as the Key Performance Indicator for a successful execution of corporate policy.

Service Intensity alludes to the marginal value of a sales associate. This metric maps how retailers can identify the optimized value of their employees.

Service Productivity

At the heart of Schedule to Demand is the empowered employee. If Service Intensity measures the workforce optimization of the store, Service Productivity evaluates the value of future performance of each sales associate. We can define Service Productivity by any measure, but the most common metric for measuring an associate is Sales per Hour (SPH).

Service Productivity defines the probability of individual performance, as a function of the specific salesperson and store operations, and is calculated with the statistics of Bayes' Theorem. In other words, Service Productivity is the probability that, for a given level of demand and customer service policy, the associate will repeat past sales performance.

The marginal value of a salesperson is calculated with the Service Productivity per associate and the Service Intensity for the store, for optimized performance and profitability.

Browsing Behavior

Shopping behavior consists of buying (what the customer purchased) and browsing (the customer behavior in the store). While retailers mine buying trends and insights from the point-of-sale data, currently there is little infrastructure to measure and monitor in real-time where the customers are inside the store, how long they stay in a specific zone, where and how long are the interactions with employees, and identifying the impact of these activities on sales. This is the uncharted territory of in-store analytics.

Browsing metrics define staying versus passing behaviors, in a zone, a department, or a section, in order to provide information on how to optimize store layout, in-store marketing, merchandising, and, of course, customer service. Specifically—

- **Occupancy Rate**: The ratio of traffic in a specific area to total traffic in the store
- **Opportunity Rate**: The number of visitors, and hence potential buyers, to a specific area.
- **Stay Time**: How long shoppers stay in a specific area in the store.
- **In Store Sales Conversion**: The ratio between transactions and visitors (Opportunity Rate) in a particular location in the store, per period of time.
- **In Store Demand**: For a specific area, demand is defined from Measured Tracking, Measured Occupancy, Calculated Occupancy, or Sampled Opportunities.

While mystery shoppers and customer surveys provide value, too many operational decisions are based on a relatively small sample of biased opinions. Counting technologies provide 24/7 view of activities and vendors are actively working on developing reasonably priced, in-store solutions. In addition to having the methodology and technology to measure in-store activities, the "soft" benefit is that much of corporate and local store perceptions dissolve in the face of hard data.

Queue Management

The checkout process is the "last touch point" in the customer experience, and frontline payroll can be from 20% to 60% of labor costs, which makes queue management important to store operations. Yet, many retail executives are reluctant to spend the organizational energy for optimization, and succumb to treating the frontline either as a "cost skeleton" or as the "staff to the max" versions.

Queue Management monitors queue behavior in real-time, and provides data on how many people are standing in line per period of time, and for how long. Queue and frontline service solutions take multiple formats due to queue behavior, store layout and other physical constraints, and objectives of the Customer Service Model.

Queue Management highlights include—

- Customer Service Models for queue comprise solutions such as "One in Front (1+1)"; Five-Five Rule"; "Serve 90% of Customers in less than 3 Minutes"; and "No Queue".
- Queues can be classified into three categories, Linear, Parallel and Unstructured.
- Frontline Management formats include Main Bank, Double-Deck, Duplex and Hubs.
- Queue behaviors include group, in-Transaction, directional, and passing versus standing.

Queue counting models, measuring the number of "waiting" customers, compare Target Lanes to the Actual Active Lanes, for Over-Staffing, Under-Staffing, and Optimal Staff Levels. Queue models that deploy "Waiting Time" are the cutting edge techniques for workforce optimization. Customer Service Models take Wait Time in context with other productivity metrics such as Transaction Time and Idle Time, for a robust, data-analytics view of store operations.

Predictive Scheduling

Predictive Scheduling is the real-time management of a bricks-and-mortar store by redeployment of available labor resources. While the technology was developed for supermarkets, it is adaptable to any bulk service points in organizations from specialty retailers to hotels and airports.

Predictive Scheduling is primarily a frontline service application, which predicts how many cashiers should be open in order to prevent the formation of queues, and manage the checkouts according to the

Customer Service Model. The optimization objective is to minimize the Idle Time, which occurs when employees maximize capacity without harming customer service.

Analytics and Deployment are two conditions that go hand-in-hand, and one cannot exist without the other for Predictive Scheduling to be meaningful to store operations. For real-time alerts and deployment policies to work, we should know not only what to do, but also what *can* we do. This is where skills, training and aligning incentives of employees come to play.

With effective Predictive Scheduling, the level of service is less sensitive to demand; the service level stays consistent, regardless of the number of customers.

THE SMALL WORLD OF RETAIL

In the context of Behavior Analytics and Schedule to Demand, the retail store relates to the physical place of business selling goods or services. This implies the site is operated by the employees of the organization. While the formats and the nature of the customers in retail stores are diverse as far as goods, services, locations, and markets go, our emphasis is on the common challenges of measuring customers and staff activities and optimizing store operations by positioning employees where they can maximize the customer experience.

To illustrate Schedule to Demand and our examples of Customer Service Models, imagine an open-air shopping mall located on the outskirts of a big metropolis, next to a cluster of business centers, and within walking distance from the train station. Our shopping mall contains Hello, a store of the retailer Special, Yellow is a department store, and Big Foodie and Little Foodie are supermarkets.

Hello sells apparel, shoes and accessories. The regular schedule consists of 4 to 8 employees, whose tasks include the fulfillment of goods from the delivery dock to the shelves, sorting merchandize, placing and changing price tags, customer service in the sense of answering questions, and manning the checkout counters as needed. In Hello store, one percent increases in conversion from browsers to buyers improves sales by more than five points.

Hello and its sister Goodbye, at the nearby suburb, belong to a chain of stores we will name Special Chain. Our sample of 50 stores will provide ample insights and tidbits into comparing stores.

Next to Hello is Yellow, a big department store. As a household brand name, people come to Yellow to shop. This destination store sells household items such as bedding, bath and home goods, but the profitable area is the newly minted electronics department. Between the warehouse and sales floor activities, Yellow has about 50 employees on site.

Down the road is Big Foodie, a high-volume supermarket with more than 3,000 daily visitors. Big Foodie payroll is heavily tilted to manning the frontline checkouts, including 30 main bank tills, 5 express lanes, 8 self-checkout kiosks, and a customer service desk with 6 stations and a linear queue that can be quickly catapulted to 25 impatient customers.

Little Foodie is a metro supermarket. Located close to the train station, Little Foodie has spikes of high-volume traffic of people shopping after work and during lunch time for a few items. It has 3 cashier stations, located close to each other at the front of the store.

Customer Service Models are a tapestry of metrics that define what, where, and when to measure activities, whose behaviors should we monitor and what do they mean, and forecasting the needs, requirements and productivity of the store and its employees. Our fictional stores will follow us as we explore in detail each facet of the Customer Service Model.

KEY POINTS

- Schedule to Demand deals with the common challenges of measuring customers and employee activities and optimizing store operations by positioning employees where they can maximize the customer experience.
- Customer Service Models are diagrams of how the retailer perceives the interaction with a customer, based on business objectives, and translated into actionable metrics.
- The customer experience in a bricks-and-mortar store has three core phases—entry, browsing and checkout.
- Scheduling to transaction creates a self-fulfilling process for missed sales opportunities.
- Key Performance Indicators include Sales Opportunities, Sales Conversion, Service Intensity, Service Productivity, Browsing Behaviors, Queue Management and Predictive Scheduling.

CHAPTER 2
SALES OPPORTUNITIES

The sales cycle in a bricks-and-mortar store starts when a potential customer physically enters the store. Measuring demand offers insights into when, where and how many people enter, exit and stay inside the store, what is the value of a potential customer, how effective are marketing promotions and campaigns in driving visitors to the stores, and how to improve communications between the local stores and corporate. Retailers deploy demand analytics in many applications, from designing store layouts, scheduling and forecasting labor resources, to real-time management. Since the number of visitors to the store is a metric of actual demand, retailers define traffic as the Key Performance Indicator (KPI) for sales opportunities.

DEFINING DEMAND

Schedule to Demand performs two functions. We track the fluctuations of demand first by location and then as a period of time. Therefore in a bricks-and-mortar store, Demand refers to sales opportunities. We should consider Demand in context with other metrics such as Sales Conversion, which sometimes requires measuring traffic, not in terms of people entering the store, but rather as people leaving the store, or the customer service metric of Service Intensity. Just as companies measure the number of website visitors or the call center callers as a step in the process of service, counting the number of people entering the retail store is the beginning of the actual sales cycle.

Demand has three key metrics:

Arrivals: The key demand metric counts how many people enter a specific store, per period of time. The Arrivals metric monitors the beginning of the sales cycle, and is deployed as the primary measurement for Sales Conversion and Service Intensity calculations. Vendors also refer to demand metrics as Patrons or Visitors, or even as a generic Traffic.

In Schedule to Demand, the sales cycle starts with Arrivals and ends with Buyers, while all people (excluding staff) inside the store are Customers.

Exiting: The metric of Exiting, measured as the number of people leaving the store or crossing the threshold of the store's entrances, can also serve as a function of demand. Easily available video and thermal technologies provide bi-directional counting data, and therefore we can measure the exit rate empirically.

There is an on-going debate whether sales conversion should be calculated against the time the customer enters the store or when he is actually leaving. We will discuss the merits of both methods later.

Occupancy: Occupancy is simply how many people are in the store, in a specific point of time. This is an important metric for train stations, restaurants, shopping malls and other facilities that have limitations of maximum occupancy. Occupancy is also used for in-store metrics.

Current period occupancy is calculated as the previous period occupancy plus number of arrivals minus number of people exiting. For example, if there were 25 people in the store at 10am, 50 people entered the store and 45 people left during the next hour, than the occupancy at 11am is 30 (25+50-45=30) potential customers.

Current Occupancy = Previous Period Occupancy + Entering - Exiting

The same calculation holds true whether the period is 15 minutes, one hour or one day. In situations where occupancy is important, best practice deploys a rolling average for the required period of time.

Door-counting ignited the market of People Counting, and most current technologies are accurate enough for counting people in motion. Typically mounted above the entrance doors, most vendors provide the minimum 90% consistent, bi-directional accuracy, and therefore Schedule to Demand models provide valid enough conclusions. Once counting companies started to guarantee 95% plus accuracy in reasonable pricing, door-counting entered mainstream retail.

The Value of Volume
Demand trends run the gamut and their nature depends on a variety of factors, starting with the type of retailer. Generally, there are destination stores such as supermarkets and the household name Big Box stores where people come with the intent to buy. Then there are specialty retailers where sales conversion plays a significant role. Each segment of retail has its own traits when it comes to what is the ideal traffic volume, but if we take the wider frame, there are 3 traffic levels: low volume stores

with fewer than 150 daily visitors, mid-level traffic hovering around 1,000 daily visitors, and high-volume stores.

Traffic influences the nature of the store. Low traffic stores tend to sell specialties, such as jewelry or niche apparel. They are also destination stores in the sense that if a potential customer enters the store, the intent to buy is high, and personal service by employees also encourages buying. Hence in low volume stores the Sales Conversion is high and Service Productivity per employee plays a dominant role.

On the other side of the spectrum, the high volume stores tend to be destination Big Box stores selling general merchandize or mall stores with transient traffic from the parking lots to the mall. With over 1,000 daily visitors, most stores have the "come, browse and buy" business model, which depends somewhat on branding and primarily on low prices.

The most interesting developments in retail today are those stores with mid-level traffic volumes that combine branding, pricing and service strategies in order to differentiate themselves; a store-within-a-store business models, digital marketing, handheld checkout devices, and, finally, a closer look at the value of employees. All of these requirements pushed the mid-volume stores to provide personalized service and at the same time stock enough inventories to accommodate customers. This paradox drives the push for behaviors measurement to and inside the store.

The first step in a door-counting project, however, is to ask does the store generate the demand as forecasted by corporate planners. If not, the retailer should investigate why, and then pursue how to increase the volume of traffic.

In one project, the corporate manager was stunned to find that one store had 30% less traffic than expected in a prime downtown location. An inquiry found that the entrance to the store was hidden due to the location of the store within the strip mall. The chain erected a tall sign with the logo of the chain at the entrance to the open mall, just off the main street. After three weeks of a dedicated marketing campaign, traffic levels reached the forecasted levels.

Another retailer was surprised to find that a store located next to a stadium experienced a drop in traffic during big events. In the hour before the event people flooded the crossway but they did not enter the retail store. Moreover, the crowd scared the regular customers away. The enterprising store manager arranged for a pre-game special to entice the early crowd to check out the store.

In a different project, a store faced the challenge of a significant drop in sales because a competitor opened a store directly on the other side of the mall, or so said the store manager. That proved to be incorrect as the traffic stayed the same. The store manager was replaced and sales increased.

Within a chain, demand trends depend on the volume of traffic, demographics, geography, and the location of the store. A mall store and a stand-alone store of the same retailer have different trends. A store in Hong-Kong is not a store in San Francisco. Even the in relatively close proximity of South Florida, the store in Boca Raton will behave somewhat differently than the same store in West Palm Beach. Creating the baseline of demand behavior, per store, per store type, and for the chain, is the first step in any analysis.

Another step in building a baseline of behavior defines the patterns of the average store. Too many retailers rank stores from top to bottom and focus on the high, low and average information. Yet, identifying ranges of behaviors provide better answers.

Figure 2-1, for example, displays a scatter point chart of Traffic and Sales Conversion for our sample of 50 stores from Special Chain. Instead of calculating the Average, we use the statistics of standard deviation, which points to a range of demand. 38 stores are in a range of 1 standard deviation from the mean, and they ran 3,100 to 4,600 weekly visitors (mid-level traffic volumes).

Figure 2-1 Traffic and Sales Conversion for 50 Stores

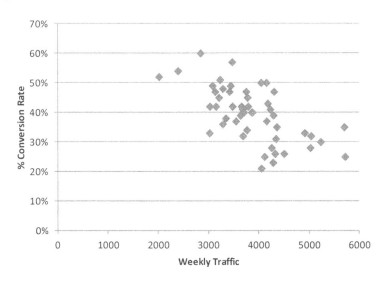

Since the Sales Conversion and Service Intensity metrics tend to be impacted by the traffic volume, the retailer can build a strategy for 38 out of the 50 stores, and treat outlier stores as exceptions.

For most retailers, demand trends are rather consistent. For apparel retailers, traffic on weekends is higher than weekdays. For stores selling baby clothes and strollers, traffic increases between 2pm to 4pm when mothers have the time to walk around. For an office supplier, weekdays are busier than the weekends in stores located where business customers dominate. For home improvement stores, contractors show up on Mondays morning while the garden hobbyists flood the store on Sundays. Jewelry sales tend to peak on Friday afternoons.

Once the retailer identifies a stable baseline, the question always arises as to why we should not move the traffic-counters to another store and save some money. Measuring traffic to build the baseline of demand is just a first step; it is the 24/7 monitoring that transforms Schedule to Demand into an operational tool.

Nuances in Demand Trends

While comparing store performance will be covered later, we should introduce a couple of rules of how to compare traffic trends among periods of time.

The first rule is to focus on weekly comparison. Typically, each day of the week has its own quirks, and while daily reports are a must for store managers, the best practice is to compare performance among stores with a week-to-week focus.

Second, beware of comparing the current period to same period in the previous year. It may sound straight forward to compare current week number 29 to the previous year week number 29, but the weather and the timing of holidays have a funny way of intruding on the analysis.

One example was the big blizzard during January 2011. Many stores faced much diminished traffic, and even closed for days, as the storm moved across the Northeast. A straight strict comparison of a 45% drop in traffic would distort the nature of year-over-year store performances. In such cases, retailers can do nothing, can modify the raw data, or can change the reporting information. Either way, the process should be discussed, and approved, by the relevant executives.

Typical errors in analysis occur when holidays shift dates. For example in 2008, Easter Sunday was on March 23. In 2009, the holiday was celebrated three weeks later on April 12. Since the impact of the holiday can last from two to six weeks, and are usually accompanied by marketing campaigns, the comparison should start from the holiday's date backwards.

People counting applications provide endless levels and views of comparisons, but sometimes less is more. While I advocate defining the Customer Service Model as a precursor to receiving data, it is prudent to return to the model once actual information flows in and adapt the original metrics to actual demand trends.

Counting Employees

Traffic counters capture the behaviors of all people, including employees. While video technologies do a good job differentiating between adults and children by height, and one company even masters the group behavior anomalies in door-counting, the ability to differentiate between customers and employees is still on the wish list. As a result, including the associates who enter and exit the store in the traffic counts, distorts the exact number of potential customers.

For many retailers, the behavior of employees is consistent enough to be part of the demand trend. This assumption is sufficient if the employees enter the stores before shifts and exit when they are done for the day, and if the staff uses a back door, and if there are two doors and the employees use only the exit door. Therefore, in some cases, we can ignore the bias in the actual counts and focus on the changes in demand.

The obvious question is why should we not factor out the employees, estimate the percentage of staff movements and deduct the estimate from the actual count. When we factor, we assume the behavior of employees is consistent in every location, for every period of time. While the behavior of employees can be consistent over time, this is not the case when we employ the raw data in 15 minute increments or real-time. The bias distorts the calculations of Sales Conversion or Service Intensity if the number of arrivals is 100 in peak hours or 20 people at closing. Factoring cements employees' behavior as a specific percent and therefore is not recommended.

Store managers always question the accuracy of the system because of the inclusions of employees. And yet focusing on trends is a better solution than factoring. One memorable remark came from an enthusiastic store manager who pronounced the staff counted how many times during the day they entered and exited the store, including bio-breaks and smoking hideouts, and therefore the counts should deduct the daily traffic number by exactly 44!

Including employees in the counts becomes an issue when helping customers, including walking in and out of the store with carts, is a standard fare. Unfortunately, for retailers where staff behaviors vary widely and are inconsistent throughout the day, door-counting, on its own merits, is irrelevant.

While changes in behavior or layout of technology can reduce counting of the staff, the solution, as most vendors are duly aware, is to find a technological resolution. Either way, the impact of counting staff should be identified and clearly discussed with the retailer during the proof-of-concept phase.

Behavior Anomalies

Behavior anomalies can pose challenges to the accuracy of the count. In luxury stores, for example, it is typical to post a guard at the main entrance. In addition to security duties, the guard also opens and closes the door for customers, especially in high-street stores located in cold climates. Since the movements of the guard may not be a complete entry or exiting behaviors, most premium counting technologies can identify and discard the guard's counts.

Another typical challenge to accurate counts occurs when a display or a rack is positioned close to the entrance and customers hover around the counting zone. For this behavior, the counts can be adjusted by separating between passing and standing behaviors. Also, by identifying the length and direction of motion, a technology can pin point a customer who walks by the entrance area and a person who actually enters or exits.

The ability to deal with behavior anomalies is a key differentiator among vendors.

THE VALUE OF A CUSTOMER

Customer Value is the ratio of Sales to Traffic, or the monetary value of an opportunity as defined by a potential customer entering the store and the average sales. While Comparable Sales metric is a testimony to management success and Sales Conversion measures the operational productivity, Customer Value is an actionable metric because it is simple—it is a sales objective for the associate.

A newly hired sales associate can easily understand that each potential customer entering the store is an average sales opportunity of, say, $10. If there is no sale with that first individual, the associate knows that to keep up with quota, the sale from the second person must be at least $20.

Figure 2-2 expands this story a bit. The objective of our Hello sample store is to sell at least $450 an hour, for an average of 30 visitors. If there are 3 employees in the store, each sales associate knows their quota is $150 Sales per Hour. For $450 sales and 30 visitors, the Customer Value is $15.

Figure 2-2 Hello Store—Customer Value

Employee	Visitors per Hour	Transactions per Hour	Sales per Hour	Average Sale	Customer Value
Abby	10	4	$148	$37	$15
Jane	10	3	$123	$41	$12
Rachel	10	3	$191	$64	$19
Totals	30	10	$462	$46	$15

For Customer Value of $15, each person who walks into the store is a $15 sales opportunity. If the sale does not happen, then the next customer is worth $30 ($15+$15=$30) for the store to keep up with the quota. If 1 out of 3 potential customers turns into a buyer, than the average sale must be at least $45 ($15+$15+$15=$45).

In the Hello store, Abby's average sale is only $37 but she had 4 customers and therefore was just below her individual quota of $150. Jane averaged $41 per sale and served only 3 customers, which brought $123 per hour. Rachel, however, served only 3 customers but with average sale of $64, she sold $41 more than the $150 quota and raised total sales for the store.

In designing performance goals for sales associates, the metrics of Customer Value (value of a sales opportunity) and Service Productivity (value of sales per associate) are interconnected. Customer Value combines information on both traffic and sales; therefore in Schedule to Demand, this metric points to the *quality* of the sales opportunity.

THE VALUE OF MARKETING

Bringing customers to the store is the job for the marketing department. While Behavior Analytics dominates marketing, information mined from the point-of-sale systems reflects buying behaviors, and therefore does not measure the activities of those who did not buy. While measuring activities provides insights on in-store activities, simply counting how many people entered the store can add further insights. The marketing department can measure the effectiveness of their promotions and campaigns by monitoring the changes in demand.

Identifying Changes in Demand

From a marketing perspective, the impact of a campaign should be felt both as an increase in traffic (more people) and an increase in the basket size (more buying). The most obvious correlation is the direct impact—the promotion launched on Sunday leads to an increase in traffic on Monday. Sadly, data does not always work out so clear cut. The trick is finding the impact on traffic while keeping other variables the same.

One aspect is comparing the impact day-to-day, such as the current Monday to the previous Monday. Another factor takes into account that the impact may take a couple of days, and may last more in one store rather than the other. A national television campaign may influence California stores by 5% while hardly moving sales in Chicago. Newspaper inserts may work in Florida but not in New York City, while emails work really well in both. And then, there is always the weather . . .

The Value of Marketing

As marketing professionals know, a key challenge is how to translate the value of a promotion or a campaign into a monetary dimension. While a sale is a function of many factors—merchandizing, operations, service etc.—traffic is a metric of demand, well suited for direct measuring of marketing.

The direct correlation between a campaign and traffic can be seen in the increase in demand. The net impact of marketing is the simple formula of the revenue from the increase in traffic minus the marketing cost as the profit from the promotion.

Net Impact of Marketing Campaign = Added Sales—Marketing Costs

However, the direct method does not portray the whole story since marketing is not only about increasing traffic, but also about providing incentives for customers to come back. Retailers have long known that frequent customers are the most profitable ones, and therefore we should assess marketing costs in terms of all visitors.

Marketing Cost Per Sales Opportunity = Marketing Campaign Cost / Visitors

And of course, there is always the question, if we did not do this marketing campaign or come out with this pricing promotion, what will it mean to our business. Sometimes the most viable insight comes from what the data does not show. With traffic data, the analytical marketing departments measure results, test theories, and compare performance by location, and per period of time.

KEY POINTS

- Demand serves as the Key Performance Indicator for Sales Opportunities.
- Demand is defined as the number of Arrivals, Exiting and Occupancy, per period of time.
- Behavior anomalies, such as employee counting, impact the accuracy of the counting.
- Customer Value provides an easy-to-explain metric of sales opportunity per visitor.
- Marketing success can be defined by changes in traffic per location and period of time.

CHAPTER 3
SALES CONVERSION

Sales Conversion is the driving force behind the admission of counting technologies to mainstream retail systems. Conversion rate has become a popular metric because it answers a simple question—how many browsers are converted to buyers?

Sales Conversion is a metric of store performance. At the store level, retailers measure the outcome of performance by Comparable Sales (Comp Sales); in other words, for the same stores, how much did our revenue grow year-over-year. Retail sales are driven by many components that build on the customer's intent to buy; branding, marketing, layout, inventory, and customer service, to name a few. Sales Conversion, however, is a metric directly correlated with the actual demand and specific environment inside the local store.

Like most simple statements, the Sales Conversion metric hides a complexity, leading to a plethora of analytical applications and counting technologies. This chapter will present the core principles of Sales Conversion, including guidelines of calculating and evaluating the Sales Conversion metric, and then, address the challenges and methodology of comparing store performance.

WHAT IS SALES CONVERSION

The sales cycle starts when a visitor enters the store and the outcome of this opportunity manifests itself in the point-of-sale system in the form of a transaction. Therefore, the Sales Conversion metric is a straight forward percentage of how many transactions to how many visitors, per period of time.

% Sales Conversion = Transactions / Visitors

For example, if there are 1,000 daily visitors and 175 transactions, then the Daily Sales Conversion is 17.5% (175/1000=17.5). As we will see, there are guidelines to calculating the conversion rate.

The benefits of measuring Sales Conversion become apparent rather quickly once the retailer rolls out the traffic counting technology. As depicted in Figure 3-1, a typical baseline of Demand and Sales Conversion behaviors point to inconsistencies in performance.

Figure 3-1 Visitors, Transactions and Sales Conversion

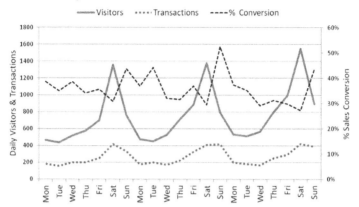

We observe in the three weeks of data, for example, Saturdays have the highest daily traffic during the week, with a lower Sales Conversion. On Sundays, the Sales Conversion is much higher than the base behavior. The third weekend saw an increase in traffic, yet the transactions barely budged, which means the increase in demand did not translate into increase in sales.

The most common facet of behavior in a retail store is the inverse correlation between traffic and Sales Conversion. In other words, when traffic increases, Sales Conversion tends to go down.

About a year or two after the roll-out, the direct result of a successful counting project is a flat conversion rate (a linear horizontal line). If Sales Conversion is constant, it means the store is able to recognize and adapt to fluctuating demand.

There are many reasons why Demand and Sales Conversion are inversely correlated. The key cause is customer service, whether inside the store during the browsing phase, or during the checkout process. More traffic also means more customers to serve, which translates to less attention per customer, more customers waiting at the frontline, and all other aspects of customer service. Another factor relates to the feelings of being "crowded", which discourages customers to stay. Over-crowding has cultural and safety implications on the shopping experience, but it also plays a role in not having the merchandise on the shelves.

During the proof-of-concept phase, retailers learn how to identify missed sales opportunities. While we will see some examples in later chapters, the process centers on the divide between visitors to transactions. Each individual who leaves without buying is considered a missed opportunity for that specific visit. As the bricks-and-mortar store become just one node in an omni-channel world, the shopping experience plays an important role in branding, wherever the sale originated.

The primary tenet of Schedule to Demand is to minimize, and even prevent, the inverse correlation between traffic and conversion. This empowers the store to perform, despite fluctuations in traffic. Actionable metrics, such as Target Sales Conversion, are defined in the Customer Service Model.

Sales Conversion is also known as the Close Rate or Capture Rate, but these terms are typically used in particular circumstances such as mall stores. The most commonly used terms are the Conversion Rate (CR) or Sales Conversion.

Guidelines to Sales Conversion

Calculating the Sales Conversion, first and foremost, must adhere to timing. Therefore, the daily conversion should be calculating with daily transactions to daily visitors, weekly transactions to weekly visitors, and so on. The reason is consistency.

Going back to our 3 week sample in Figure 3-1, the weekly conversion rate is not the average of the daily Sales Conversion at 36%, but calculated as the weekly transactions to weekly visitors at 35%. Following the guideline of timing, the conversion rate for the weekdays is 33%, Saturday at 27% and Sunday at 44%. As we can see, even in a limited set of data, rounding and other bias can vary the calculation. Therefore, it is best to always calculate the Sales Conversion from the sum of the data in the distinct period of time.

Arrivals versus Exiting

The debate over which metric—Arrivals or Exiting—better represents demand in Sales Conversion calculations, typically erupts at two to three weeks after the installation of the sensors and once the data starts flowing in. Since managers involved in the decision process tend to spend an enormous amount of energy and time debating the merits of each metric, it is time, we, as an industry, should reach common guidelines.

History favors Arrivals. Since the sales cycle starts when a person enters the store, the concept of conversion relates to performance in context with actual opportunities. The Arrivals metric works when the average staying time in the store is less than 30 minutes and, as a result, the reports can best capture the hourly, 4-hour periods, and daily conversion rates.

In addition, by capturing the arrivals data starting at the opening hour, we limit the inclusion of employees, as those often show up to work before the store opens. Many stores have displays or signs outside the official store entrance line. By cutting the counts after closing time, we limit the inclusion of employees going in and out, as they close the store for the day.

Exiting gained favor as the metric of choice for conversion calculations as retailers started asking how to impact the Sales Conversion and all fingers pointed to scheduling. Once we embarked on the road to adapt customer service and frontline checkouts to actual demand, measuring the outcome by Sales Conversion made much more sense if we tied people leaving the store and people buying, in the same period of time. We will delve into the metrics of scheduling to demand later, but here, suffice it to say that, yes, the exiting metric works better for real-time management.

My rule of thumb for Sales Conversion calculations is to apply Arrivals for reporting purposes and Exiting for the 15-minute scheduling requirements.

Defining Transactions

Anyone who has dealt with raw data from the point-of-sale system can attest to its complexity and variety. For Sales Conversion, the core point-of-sale metric is a transaction. While the number of items and the average basket size are important factors in understanding the composition of sales, the transaction data field for Sales Conversion indicates the total sale for a Single Buying Unit.

In Sales Conversion calculations, the transaction represents a sale. Therefore these challenges arise:

Returns: Returning merchandise has direct impact on sales, but the return activity is not a part of the store performance in that particular period of time. Therefore returns should not be included in Sales Conversion calculations.

Exchanges: To include exchanges or not, poses a more difficult dilemma because the customer had obviously spent time in the store and therefore was influenced by what was happening in the store at the time of the exchange. However, the sale originated at the initial transaction.

If we want to be accurate, we should take out the original transaction and add the current one, but this requires re-calculation of past performance. For most retailers, the impact of exchanges on transactions is not substantial and is usually consistent, and therefore they are best ignored.

Timing of the sale: Buying a sweater is a straight forward sale. Buying a refrigerator is not. Most electronics stores require a deposit when the order is made, but the product is delivered a couple of days later. While those among us who have suffered from defective merchandise or abysmal delivery service may not be happy to acknowledge, the sale *did* occur when we signed off on the order and paid the initial deposit.

Gift Certificates also pose the question—when does the sale occur. While the point-of-sale system registers the sale when we buy the gift certificate, from a customer service point of view, the sale occurs when the gift card is redeemed. Therefore, avoiding the nightmares of holiday shopping by purchasing a gift certificate means that we will measure store performance only when the teenager actually comes to the store and buys "my-mother-will-never-get-me-these-orange-shoes."

The Wonders of Regression Analysis

So far we have addressed Sales Conversion in the context of a store, but retailers tend to assess how a store is doing in context to the chain. Before we leap into comparing stores, we will consider how to address the relationships between Traffic and Sales Conversion.

Regression is a statistical technique to measure the connections between two or more phenomena, which, in our case, it is the relationship between Traffic and Sales Conversion. Regression shows that as traffic volume increases, how it impacts the Sales Conversion.

Each point on the scatter chart in Figure 3-2 is a store, with average weekly traffic on the horizontal y-axis and the average Sales Conversion on the vertical x-axis. Remember our Special Chain. For the 50 stores, the linear regression line between Traffic and Sales Conversion is 0.40. We can also say that traffic volume has 40% weight on the factors influencing the Sales Conversion.

Figure 3-2 Traffic and Sales Conversion—50 Stores

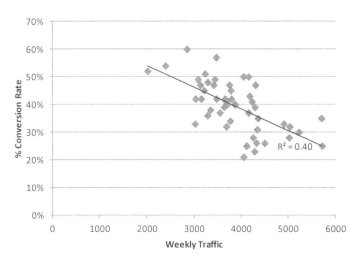

The significant influence of traffic volume on the store performance is yet another example why measuring demand should be important to retailers. The scatter point map of the Traffic and Sales Conversion provides the best birds-eye view of store performance in context to the chain.

COMPARING STORES PERFORMANCE

Many retailers include comparisons of performance in calculating compensation and bonus criteria for their managers. A common practice ranks stores from top-to-bottom by Sales Conversion rate. While sorting by traffic levels makes sense for destination stores, the close correlation of demand and conversion requires context instead of a list. The process starts with categorizing the stores by characteristics such as geography, demographics, and traffic volume. Once we identified a baseline of behaviors, the retailer can set the Target Rate.

If there is a one consistent complaint by many managers, which carries across all retail chains and stores, is that the Target Sales Conversion is considered arbitrary and is not feasible for local conditions. Retail managers argue, on the other hand, that the comparison of stores is the best way to identify the good and less performing managers and to encourage the laggards to improve. The answer includes avoiding a mad rush and setting the baseline on no less than the three months of data, and, at the same time, categorizing the stores and building a leveled Target Rate.

Since Sales Conversion plays a crucial part for specialty retailers, the following case study reflects how the process works for 50 stores. Our sample from Special Chain contains three types of stores:

- **14 stand-alone stores:** The stand-alone stores are located in plazas, and the nature of parking and the position of the store points to a destination behavior; hence the customer enters the store with the intent to buy.
- **16 open-air mall stores with a single entrance:** Open-air mall stores have a single entrance. Although our fictitious Special Chain is a household name, these stores are not considered as destination stores and therefore are subjected to the rigors of Sales Conversion.
- **20 mall stores with 2 entrances:** The mall stores have two entrances, one from inside the mall and the second entrance opens up to a parking lot. This matters, because the traffic includes also cross-over traffic, people who have no intent in visiting the store, but those who enter the store from the parking lot and walk through the store as a pass way into the mall.

For mall stores with entrances to both the mall and the parking lot the question is—can the people passing through be considered as true sales opportunities? The answer is no, and yes! From a marketing perspective, these visitors did not enter the store with the intent to buy. It means that we should treat marketing studies with caution when it comes to mall store traffic. On the other hand, by entering the store, these visitors are exposed to what the store has to offer, and therefore should be considered as a sales opportunity.

I once had a ferocious discussion with a district manager on the sales value of pass through traffic. Eventually she agreed to make internal changes in the store, and, as a result the store increase sales in a direct correlation to the increase in impulse buying.

In general, Sales Conversion in a mall store with a parking lot entrance will probably be less than a similar mall store with only mall entrances. This also means the store should be adapted to address these impulse shoppers.

Another facet of this debate refers to the destination concept. While retailers such as the Gap or Tiffany's are household names, typically they are not destination stores, in the sense that customers enjoy browsing in the stores, but many people do not come with the intent to buy. Even the pure destination stores such as Home Depot or Lowe's can have variations in the buying behaviors due to specific locations, such as standalone, or as part of a mall complex.

Urban or rural environments, upper middle class or low wage neighborhoods, dominant position or surrounded by competitors, are just some of the factors that can influence customer behaviors, and accordingly the Target Rate. A diversified retail chain can have several Target Rates.

Identify Comparison Categories

The process of comparing stores starts with categorizing the stores into broad sections of demand behaviors. Since the 50 stores carry between 2,000 to 6,000 weekly visitors and the conversion rate ranges from 20% to 60%, our fictitious Special Chain decided to start the process by looking in each type of store—standalone, open mall and mall stores.

Traffic for the 14 stand-alone stores ranged between 2,000 to 4,500 weekly visitors, yet the stores displayed consistent conversion behavior of 51% and a standard deviation of 4%. We can also say that 8 out of 14 stores had between 47% and 55% conversion rates. As we see in Figure 3-3, the standalone stores display *consistent* conversion behavior.

Behavior for the mall stores was a different story. For one, demand levels were similar for both the open (Figure 3-4) and closed (Figure 3-5) mall stores, averaging just above 4,000 weekly visitors. While the conversion rate of the open mall stores averaged 39% and for the mall stores at 34%, there were such fluctuations in the data that we could not say there is a typical behavior for each type of mall store. In this case methodology dictates we treat the open mall and closed mall stores as a single category—mall stores.

Classify Baseline Behaviors

The next phase of the comparison process defines best performers, average behavior and laggards. Once we build the store categories, we can take the analysis a step down and cobble the stores with similar characteristics such as geography and weather, demographics and household income, layout, and, of course, demand levels, as sub-categories for more "accurate" comparison.

Due to the correlation between Traffic and Sales Conversion, behavior of stores in each demand level bares close scrutiny. For example we can chose to analyze only stores with the weekly traffic of 4,000 to 5,000 visitors. In essence, by picking only stores within the demand band, we negated the impact of traffic on Sales Conversion and therefore can zero in on operational performance.

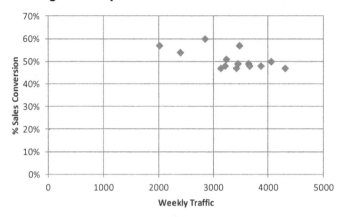

Figure 3-3 Special Chain—Standalone Stores

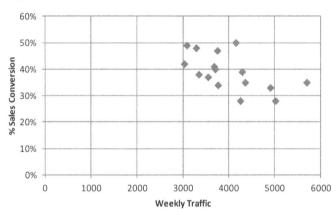

Figure 3-4 Special Chain—Mall Stores with 1 Entrance

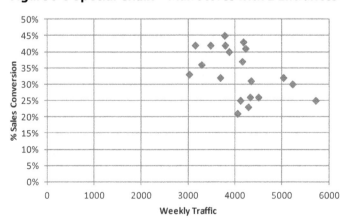

Figure 3-5 Special Chain—Mall Stores with 2 Entrances

The scatter point map of the 4 mall stores with 1 Entrance and weekly traffic of 4,000 to 5,000 visitors (Figure 3-6) spots a couple of behaviors. First, there is wide disparity of conversion rates between the top performer with 50% conversion and the store at the bottom with 21%. Since the average conversion rate is 33% we can identify the laggards as those below, say, 30% conversion. We also identify another top performer as a store with 5,000 weekly visitors and Sales Conversion of 33%, which therefore bucks the trend of more traffic less Sales Conversion. Finally, we identify the store with low traffic and low conversion of 28%. Just identifying and dealing with the laggard stores can provide a quick return on investment from a counting project.

Figure 3-6 Special Chain—4 Mall Stores, 1 Entrance

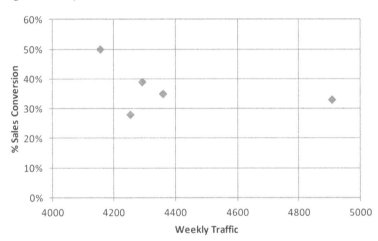

Select Conversion Targets

Three months after the roll-out and after discussions with the field managers, Special Chain defined the Sales Conversion targets. For the 50 stores, the average Sales Conversion of 40% will not work because of the wide differences in demand trends.

For the 14 stand-alone stores, with average Sales Conversion of 51% and a standard deviation of 4%, the Target Rate was the simple average of 51%. Stores were considered in good standing as long as they did not carry less than 48% Sales Conversion. In the compensation plans, bonus boosters are given to managers whose stores had 55% conversion and above.

For the mall stores, since there were too many inconsistencies in the data, the decision was to stay in a target conversion range of 30% to 40%. This helped to turn the attention to stores in the lower third of performance. The performance incentives for stores with conversion of 40% or above were devised with the intention of encouraging improvements.

For a strong push forward and to negate doubters, the first year compensation policy should focus on the self-improvement of each individual store. Once store managers learn to work with traffic and conversion data, Sales Conversion rates should be similar for stores at the same category and demand levels and therefore adequately compared.

Once the Conversion Targets are defined, we can start the phase of how to improve conversion with the key performer indicator of service, the metric of Service Intensity.

KEY POINTS

- Sales Conversion is a Key Performance Indicator for the bricks-and-mortar store, measuring the conversion rate of browsers to buyers.
- The most common facet of behavior in a retail store is the inverse correlation between Traffic and Sales Conversion; when Demand increases, Sales Conversion tends to go down.
- The recommend methodology for Sales Conversion calculations is to apply the metric Arrivals for reporting purposes and the Exiting field for the 15-minute scheduling requirements.
- Due to the correlation between demand and Sales Conversion, measure store performance and conversion rate in context to traffic, plus the chain's range of behaviors.
- Compare store performance first against itself, second against peers with similar characteristics and only then, against the chain.
- The tenet of Schedule to Demand is to minimize, and if possible prevent, the inverse connection between traffic and conversion, and empower the store to perform, regardless of fluctuations in demand.

CHAPTER 4
SERVICE INTENSITY

If Sales Conversion measures the success in converting visitors to buyers, than Service Intensity is the Key Performance Indicator of how to maximize sales opportunities. Service Intensity drives the process to increase sales. While Service Intensity may sound as yet another name for the Customers to Staff Ratio, our metric covers a more holistic method of how to schedule sales associates.

As part of the Customer Service Model, Service Intensity requires a baseline of behavior that guides corporate policy, and adds a way to measure the performance of the local store. Therefore, we need to define the parameters of Service Intensity, and, in addition, create a percentage of success, or the Service Level Measurement (SLM). The optimal ratio of customers to staff, in the sense of a balance between customer service and profitability, depends on the nature of the retailer's market segment and the marginal value of a sales associate.

WHAT IS SERVICE INTENSITY

In Schedule to Demand, Service Intensity provides retailers with guidelines on how many sales associates are required to accommodate the retailer's Customer Service Model.

Service Intensity = Customers / Associates

Service Intensity is calculated as a ratio of customers to employees, per period of time. If the value of Service Intensity is 5, it means the ratio of Visitors to Staff is 5. Service Intensity, however, can be calculated in different ways and we will examine each possible component of Customers, Associates and Period of Time metrics.

Define Customers by Demand
The simplest calculation is against the flow of traffic, or number of potential customers entering the store, hence, Arrivals, typically per hour, divided by the number of associates.

Service Intensity = Arrivals / Associates

For example, if 48 people walked into the store during the hour, and there are 4 associates on the sales floor, then the Service Intensity is 1 to 12 (48/4=12). We can also say that each associate has to service 12 potential customers, per hour. If 20 people entered the store, then each staff member can accommodate 5 customers (20/4=5).

Define the Period of Time

Service Intensity is typically calculated per hour. However as workforce systems proliferate and the forecasting moves away from excel spreadsheets into sophisticated systems that deploy bottom-up data, the schedule is now done in 15 minute increments. This opens the door for innovations.

Remember our Hello Store. In Figure 4-1 we see a sample data in 15 minute segments for Arrivals, Sales Associates, Service Intensity, and Average Service Time, for a total of 2 hours. Hello received 48 visitors between 11am to noon and then 72 additional arrivals during the next hour.

Figure 4-1 Hello Store 15 Minute and 1 Hour Periods

		PER 15 MINUTES				PER 1 HOUR				
Start Period	End Period	Arrivals	Sales People	Service Intensity	Average Service Time	Arrivals	Payroll Hours	Service Intensity	Average Service Intensity	Average Service Time
11:00	11:15	12	4	3.0	05:00					
11:15	11:30	9	4	2.3	06:40					
11:30	11:45	13	4	3.3	04:36					
11:45	12:00	14	4	3.5	04:17	48	4	12	3.0	05:00
12:00	12:15	13	4	3.3	04:36					
12:15	12:30	14	4	3.5	04:17					
12:30	12:45	24	5	4.8	03:07					
12:45	13:00	21	5	4.2	03:34	72	4.5	16	3.9	03:48

If we try to identify the lunch hour crowd, it is obvious—the traffic started to rise at 12:30pm. The regular schedule anticipated more traffic during lunchtime and our Hello store was ready with an additional sales associate, raising the number of employees on the floor from 4 to 5.

If we calculated the metrics based on hourly data, we would have ended with a Service Intensity of 12 (48/4=12) and 16 (72/4.5=16) respectively. Unfortunately, this calculation imbues behaviors, such as the Average Stay Time in the store is less than 30 minutes, rendering the metric imprecise.

We also calculated the Service Intensity for every 15 minutes, such as between 11am and 11:15am with 12 arrivals and 4 sales associates the ratio is 3 (12/4=3). Next, we calculated hourly ratios by averaging each 15 minute period, which belongs to that specific hour. The Average Service Intensity between 11am to 12pm is the ratio of 3 visitors to 1 sales associate; between 12pm to 1pm the ratio increased to 3.9. This means that, on average, each associate should have provided service to 3 customers during the first hour and almost 4 customers in the second hour.

Therefore, if the Average Staying Time in the store is somewhere between 15 to 30 minutes, then calculating the Service Intensity as an average of 15 minute ratios, paints a more authentic picture of how the store works. Using the average method works best, whether we aim for hourly or daily rate, or a longer period of time.

Digging deeper in the Hello Store data, we see that Service Intensity rose above 4 after 12:30pm. Special Chain had already learned that when Service Intensity is above 4.5 it may indicate that more help is needed. One option is calling the manager to help on the sales floor. Real-time deployment will bring the number of employees to 6. With 24 customers at the 12:45pm time segment, Service Intensity returns to 4.

Define Customers by Occupancy

For retailers with high volume traffic, such as Big Box or department destination stores, it is better to calculate Service Intensity against Occupancy rather than the Arrivals field. In large sized stores, the employees are typically scheduled per department. By calculating the store's Service Intensity with Occupancy, we keep the consistency in measuring behavior both to and inside the store.

In our Big Box store Yellow, using the Service Intensity based on Occupancy provides ratios of 5 to 7 in the first 90 minutes. At 12:30pm, the rate of Customers to Associates jumps close to 8 and as the visitors flood in, the store ends with a metric of over 12 to 1 in the last 15 minutes (Figure 4-2)

Figure 4-2 Service Intensity as function of Occupancy

Start Period	End Period	Arrivals	Exiting	Calculated Occupancy	Sales People	Service Intensity
				45		
11:00	11:15	42	35	52	10	5.2
11:15	11:30	39	36	55	10	5.5
11:30	11:45	43	37	61	10	6.1
11:45	12:00	44	48	57	10	5.7
12:00	12:15	53	58	52	10	5.2
12:15	12:30	64	55	61	10	6.1
12:30	12:45	84	68	77	11	7.0
12:45	13:00	121	75	123	12	10.3

For a Big Box store where associates do not interact with customers, the question is—why does the Service Intensity matter? It does—because crowding impacts the shopping experience. Although the store may not have a service model, there may be pockets of direct service, such as the Paint Desk in home improvement stores, or the checkout counter in the Shoe Department. In addition, as department stores play with the store-in-store business model, the flow patterns will illuminate the relationship of customers to the store and the brand.

Since the accuracy of measuring occupancy tends to suffer from technological challenges, retailers can use the Arrivals data for the 15 minute segments. For large destination stores, however, using Occupancy is a better metric. Either way, the calculation method should maintain consistency.

Defining Sales Associates
An important part of the analytics process relates to which employees should be treated as sales associates. In luxury stores, all employees on the floor are considered as sales. The same logic holds for small, destination stores, and most specialty stores. The store managers and technical support personnel should be considered according to the definition of their jobs. Working in the warehouse is not a sales job. And frontline associates have their own metrics as part of queue management.

In department stores, employees assigned to the Shoe Department function as sales associates, at least most of the time . . . What about the staff in Hardware? Do the associates help the customers, or do they spend the majority of their shifts sorting wood rails by size or shifting tools from one aisle to another. In Big Box stores, most business models do not include direct customer service and are based on customers sorting the heaps of pillows and browsing rows of clothes. The idea of thinking in terms of Service Intensity raises eyebrows, and yet the employees on the sales floor are de facto interacting with customers.

The sales process and the type of retailer play a big part in forming the optimized Service Intensity. How to calculate Service Intensity depends on how the retailer defines the Customer Service Model, and this should be discussed, and determined, before any technology is installed.

LINKING SCHEDULE TO SERVICE

Once they hear about Service Intensity, the first question most retail executives ask is what should be the optimal ratio. The value depends on the nature of the retail store and the calculation method. Using Demand, the Service Intensity of 15 makes sense for a high volume store where the tasks of the employees are to stock shelves, move clothes back and forth on racks, or endlessly change price tags. 15 is a miserable ratio if the business is service dependent. Based on limited deployments in the field, the optimal Service Intensity ratio exists from 4 to 9.

Remember our Special Chain with the 50 stores sample. We took 3 months of data, calculated the Service Intensity in 15 minute increments, and averaged the outcome to reach a baseline for each store. For all the stores in our sample, the Average Service Intensity is 5.9.

To link the schedule to service policies, we have to go farther. The process starts by learning the relationships between demand, service and conversion, and building a baseline of behaviors. Since Sales Conversion ratio displays the link between demand and transactions, and Service Intensity measures demand and service, finding the correlation between these two metrics points to optimal values. It turns out, that service and conversion have an inverse correlation as we see in Figure 4-3.

Figure 4-3 Sales Conversion and Service Intensity

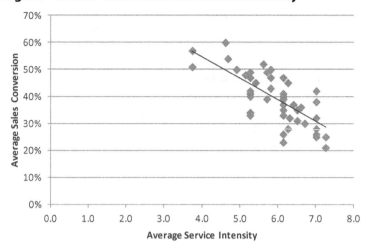

A lower Service Intensity ratio is coupled with an increase in Sales Conversion. That makes sense. When each associate serves fewer customers, and gives more attention to one customer, then we should expect an increase in revenue.

Ask any luxury retailer, and they will confide that despite the emphasis on brand, their salespeople make a difference, sometimes to the point that an experienced salesperson can double, even triple sales at the same store, same period of time, and the with the same type of merchandise. Despite perceptions—and I'll say it loud and clear—even for high-turnover, low-wage retailers, employees matter! Just ask McDonald's and Starbucks.

Average Service Time
Another way to help retailers pinpoint an optimal Service Intensity is to turn the formula around and observe the Average Service Time. For example in our Hello store, Service Intensity for 11am to 11:15am is 3. This means each associate served, on average, 3 customers. It also means during the 15 minute period, on average, the service time was 5 minutes (15/3=5).

Average Service Time per Customer = Period of Time * Service Intensity

In Figure 4-1, we saw that in Hello the Average Service Time was high as 6:40 minutes and low as 3:07. The search for an optimal service time should be taken in context with the nature and scale of the reseller's sale cycle.

Retailers use analytics in many areas, including cost studies, based on activities, such as how long does it take to stock one aisle or another, sort the warehouse, or process a transaction. This opens new areas to study, such as what is the optimal sales cycle? Or, what is the impact of the length of service on revenue?

Weighted Service Intensity

Now, we will complicate this story. Not all sales associates are the same. Moreover, in corporate planning, the quality of the schedule *does* matter.

A basic classification in workforce is between full-time employees and temporary employees. Some retailers treat a temporary employee as half a point, so if we scheduled 2 full time employees and 2 temps, the number of associates is considered 3 (1+1+0.5+0.5=3). If 12 people enter the store, then the original Service Intensity would have been 3 (12 customers / 4 associates = 3). But, Weighted Service Intensity would have been 4 (12 customers / 3 weighted associates =4).

Weighted Service Intensity is useful for retailers where service is divided between sales associates who focus on new accounts, and customer service employees who address complaints and technical issues. We can also use a variation of the Weighted Service Intensity in retailers where employees are busy with fulfillment by stocking and restocking goods on the shelves, not with customer service, and yet, their presence has an impact on sales.

Service Intensity in Mall Stores

Service Intensity is a bit more complicated to calculate in open mall stores because the sales cycle typically starts at the display outside the lease line; it matters because door-counters only measure how many people entered the store, and yet, the associate engages with the customer *before* any record of activity.

A more sophisticated counter can measure how long the customer stood in front of the display and then entered the store. This is especially important for luxury retailers since the sales cycle is long, and an average sales cycle of 45 minutes is not unheard off. When there are 3 associates on the floor, and one is occupied with a customer for almost an hour, this effectively means that the other 2 carry the burden of serving all the rest of the customers.

This impacts calculations of scheduling if the store experiences this kind of sales in specific periods, such as an increase in wedding preparations, or special holidays, or even specific sales. It also helps to understand when the store manager, typically occupied by other duties, serves in the capacity of a sales associate. This type of scheduling in mall stores requires an accurate counter, which handles both motion and staying behaviors correctly, and that's a whole different story.

SERVICE LEVEL MEASUREMENT

Service Level Measurement (SLM) is a metric of success in the Customer Service Model. It is also the key to the communication process between corporate policy and local conditions in the store. As a percentage, Service Level Measurement captures the ability of each store to perform according to a corporate policy. While Sales Conversion and Service Intensity are Key Performance Indicators on how the store *should* perform, Service Level Measurement monitors *actual* operations.

In Hello Store, between 11am to 1pm, 6 times out of 8 periods of 15 minute increments, the Service Intensity was less than 4 (Figure 4-4). If the Customer Service Model requires a ratio of 4 or fewer customers per sales associate, than the store matched the corporate policy by 80%.

Figure 4-4 Service Intensity per 15 Minute Segments

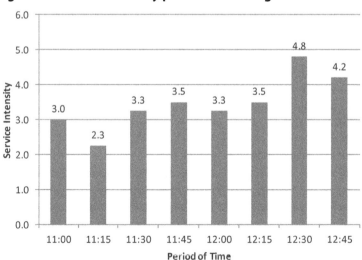

Service Level Measurement works for all Key Performance Indicators. For example, the Customer Service objective can state that the stores reach 35% or above sales conversion for at least 85% of the time. Another popular facet of this metric is in queue management, where the objectives are to achieve a maximum waiting time of, say, 3 minutes, at least 90% of the time.

Monitoring the Range of Success

For many retailers, and especially when it comes to managing Service Intensity, it is better to work with a range of success. Instead of a maximum or minimum threshold, instead of the single value of the average, retailers can define successful performance as long as the store stays within a range of one standard deviation from the average.

Standard Deviation describes the spread of the data from the average. In normal distribution, one standard deviation below and above the mean will include more than 68% of the cases. While each retailer will have its own distribution of behaviors, when it comes to Service Intensity it is best to work from the range of plus and minus one standard deviation from the average. One can also pick a "close enough" range to work with.

If we take Special Chain 50 store sample and count the number of stores within each whole point, we will see that 78% of the stores have a Service Intensity above 4 and less than 7 (Figure 4-5). In this case, the retailer should take a closer look at each of the 11 outlier stores and determine what can be done to push these stores into the range of success. This self-review process, which typically occurs during the three months following the roll-out, is one of the reasons why before any action is taken within the stores, corporate should first review, and learn, the data.

Figure 4-5 Service Intensity Levels

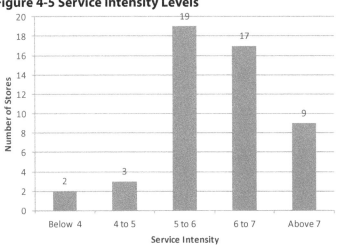

Determining the corporate Service Level Measurement is yet another component to the Customer Service Model. Beneath this process a deeper challenge exists for the retailer—what is the marginal value of adding a sales person on revenue?

THE MARGINAL VALUE OF SALES ASSOCIATE

In discovering the added value of a sales person, we look at the Sales per Hour as a productivity metric, while keeping all variables—traffic levels, period of time, matching locations—the same, and only changing how many associates are scheduled.

If the store schedules 4 people between 4pm and 5pm, what would be the impact on revenue if we scheduled 5 associates? What are the Sales per Hour for 6 employees?

These conceptual tests should be done not only during high traffic hours, but also before there is an expected increase in traffic, in order to see when it is best to start preparing for peak demand.

In the scatter chart of Figure 4-6, we correlated Sales per Hour to the number of Associates. While this is a fictional sample, the positive correlation between sales and number of employees mirrors actual projects. Adding one salesperson increases revenue, but each revenue segment is less than the previous revenue slice. This makes common sense. If demand stays at the same level, there is still natural buying behavior, limiting how much the associate can do to influence the sale.

Figure 4-6 Marginal Value of Sales Associate

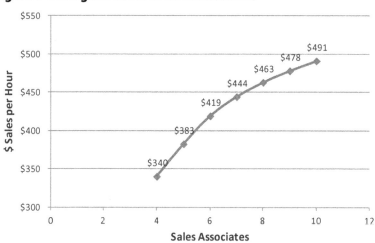

The marginal value of the a salesperson should be taken in context with Service Intensity, which is a scheduling metric, and Service Productivity, which measures individual performance. The context of the individual performance of an associate in relationship to the store's operational success is the topic of the next chapter.

KEY POINTS

- Service Intensity (SI) guides retailers on how many sales associates are needed in the store in order to accommodate the Customer Service Model.
- Service Intensity is the ratio of Customers to Sales Associates, per period of time.
- If the average staying time is somewhere between 15 to 30 minutes, then calculating the Service Intensity as an average of a 15 minute segment paints a more authentic picture of the store.
- For high volume stores, it is better to calculate Service Intensity against Occupancy rather than the Arrivals, in order to maintain consistency in scheduling for the store and each department.
- Service Intensity and Sales Conversion have an inverse correlation. As each associate serves fewer customers, giving more attention to the customer, there is an increase in revenue.
- Weighted Service Intensity allows retailers to define the type of associate, i.e. temporary or full-time, when structuring the schedule.
- Service Level Measurement (SLM) is a metric of success in the Customer Service Model. While Sales Conversion and Service Intensity are Key Performance Indicators on how the store *should* perform, Service Level Measurement monitors *actual* operations.
- The marginal value of the a salesperson should be taken in context with Service Intensity, which is a scheduling metric, and Service Productivity, which measures individual performance.

CHAPTER 5
SERVICE PRODUCTIVITY

At the heart of Schedule to Demand is the empowered employee. Targeting individual customers or Personalization is all the rage in what retailers must do. While custom marketing and individual pricing to each potential customer is a competitive advantage, in the environment of the bricks-and-mortar store, employees play an important role in the sales process. To optimize performance, it is not enough just to schedule according to the retailer's Customer Service Model, but also to ensure the employees are trained, empowered and motivated to succeed.

In Schedule to Demand, Service Intensity guides the performance of the physical store, and Service Productivity is the metric of productivity for each sales associate.

WHAT IS SERVICE PRODUCTIVITY

Service Productivity is the predicted value of a sales associate. Current scheduling methodology uses data on availability, job position, and skills to assign a particular employee to a specific time and location. Our objective is to include a predictive function of the associate's productivity in the forecasting process. Service Productivity, in other words, is the probability, for a given level of traffic and service policy, the salesperson will repeat past sales performance.

Sales associates are typically measured by Sales per Hour. The nature of the sales cycle sometimes makes it challenging to assign a specific transaction to an individual sales associate. However, the retailers can build a matrix of performance based on; how many employees are assign to the store; the length of the shifts; the number of transactions and sales information. In fact, many retailers do so in order to assign and compensate by commission. For simplicity sake, we will assume a direct link between transaction and the sales associate.

MEASURING PERFORMANCE PER ASSOCIATE

If the Key Performance Indicator for sales performance is Sales per Hour (SPH), our first step builds the baseline of performance per employee. Back in Hello Store, we identified our 5 sales associates—Abby, Bobby, Jane, Rachel, and Mike who joined them in the last 30 minutes. Our staff sold $1,083 worth of clothes and accessories to 12 customers out of the 48 visitors who walked into the store between 11am to 12pm (See Figure 5-1). Abby has 4 transactions, which means she serviced and sold to 4 customers, the most transactions per hour. Jane only sold to 2 customers but achieved the highest Average Sale $161. Another way of looking at the data is Abby had the highest conversion rate at 12% (4 buyers / 48 visitors = 12%), and Jane was the most productive employee with hourly sales totaling $321.

Figure 5-1 Hello Store Employees—2 Hour Period

	11:00 to 12:00				12:00 to 13:00		
Staff	Trans-actions	$ Sales per Hour	$ Average Sale	Staff	Trans-actions	$ Sales per Hour	$ Average Sale
Abby	4	$248	$62	Abby	5	$303	$61
Bob	3	$223	$74	Bob	3	$201	$67
Jane	2	$321	$161	Jane	3	$296	$99
Mike	0	$0	$0	Mike	1	$81	$81
Rachel	3	$291	$97	Rachel	3	$276	$92
Totals	12	$1,083	$90	Totals	15	$1,157	$77
Hourly Traffic			48	Hourly Traffic			72
Hourly Conversion Rate			25%	Hourly Conversion Rate			21%

In the second hour, the same patterns emulated the sales behaviors. Abby sold to 5 customers. Jane had the higher average sale at $99. The store manager describes Abby as the salesperson with a knack for selling hot items, while Jane excels in encouraging customers to add accessories to the dress. In Schedule to Demand terminology, Abby converts more browsers to buyers, and Jane generates more sales from customers. In Behavior Analytics, the objective is to identify the balance between conversion and productivity—and how can the retailer optimize the schedule.

In the second hour we also see the influence of the inverse correlation between the traffic and sales conversion. While traffic almost doubled compare to the first hour, the sales conversion went down from 25% to 21%. Since the store anticipated a surge in demand, they had added a fifth employee. Mike started his shift at 12:30pm and closed 1 sale in his first 30 minutes of work. Looking closer, we can see the inverse relationship between the number of employees and marginal value, as the store's Average Sale went down from $90 to $77. In fact, average sale for each one of our original 4 employees was lower in the second hour.

Another facet of the inverse correlation between number of employees and their marginal value, translates into lower Average Sale when the Service Intensity increases. In Hello Store, the first hour had an Average Sale of $90, and Service Intensity of 3. In the second hour, the store had an Average Sale of $77 and the Service Intensity is almost 4.

By averaging the sales performance in these two periods, we can create a baseline of performance for these two hours (Figure 5-2). For a stable sample of data, baseline performance should be based, at a minimum, on a rolling 3 months of data. We calculated baseline performances for each of our five associates in Hello Store, for an average sale of $71.

Figure 5-2 Baseline vs. 2 Hour Performances

2 Hour - Performance By Employee				Baseline Performance By Employee			
Staff	Trans-actions	$ Sales per Hour	$ Average Sale	Staff	Trans-actions	$ Sales per Hour	$ Average Sale
Abby	4.5	$276	$61	Abby	4	$245	$61
Bob	3	$212	$71	Bob	3	$186	$71
Jane	2.5	$309	$130	Jane	3	$253	$130
Mike	0.5	$41	$41	Mike	3	$198	$66
Rachel	3	$284	$95	Rachel	3	$261	$95
Totals	13.5	$1,120	$83	Totals	16	$1,143	$71

The Performance Range for an Associate

While the Average is a simple metric to understand and work with, to predict future performance it is better to use a range of performance. The probability of reaching a specific hourly sale level of $200 is very low, but a range between $180 and $220 makes more sense. Since we desire to find a range below and above the average, we can assume normal distribution and use the statistics of Standard Deviation as thresholds for performance. Therefore, for Service Productivity, we will treat performance as the Standard Deviation from the Average Sale per Hour range.

Rachel, for example, worked 75 days in the last 3 months. In Figure 5-3, we see her Average Sales per Hour for each working day. For simplicity we look at the daily average sale, but a sophisticated analytics program can take this process deeper by pinpointing performance per reporting period of time, using a 4 hour period. For our purposes, Rachel's average sale per hour productivity is $261.

Figure 5-3 Rachel's Sales per Hour—Baseline

$233	$259	$253	$251	$250
$251	$225	$231	$232	$230
$231	$230	$244	$241	$254
$237	$236	$251	$242	$245
$238	$246	$254	$248	$250
$256	$248	$257	$256	$266
$261	$254	$277	$256	$278
$261	$256	$278	$256	$250
$262	$266	$279	$262	$257
$264	$266	$278	$268	$257
$271	$268	$282	$273	$259
$272	$270	$284	$276	$260
$275	$273	$285	$285	$262
$289	$278	$287	$287	$271
$291	$284	$290	$291	$272

If we had to predict how often Rachel's hourly sales will be exactly $261, we will end up with a very low probability. It will also be a meaningless number, because our objective is to find a metric that will describe performance, not a specific sale. If, however, we calculate Rachel's Standard Deviation of $17, add and subtract the Standard Deviation from the Average, we can say that Rachel's baseline performance should be between $244 to $278 Sales per Hour (Figure 5-3, highlighted cells). As long as the store's environment stays the same, the salesperson should perform consistently to baseline.

Currently, much of the scheduling process is done at the store level, typically with Comparable Sales metrics. One of the advantages of a workforce system, is the ability to build the forecasting from the bottom up, starting from individual performance. If Hello Store's quota is based on $1,100 per hour, with our five associates, we can forecast the more accurate revenue at $1,143 (Figure 5-2).

In the real world, this forecasting method is new and therefore should be tested, and integrated, slowly into the organization. Some people will object on the grounds that this is "too subjective" and does not take into account variables such as weather, merchandize, and number of employees. Yet a more accurate forecast improves management. As long as the frontline employees have the ability to access, review and address the data, communications of store and corporate will improve.

This is not the end of the story. Calculating future productivity requires addressing the factors of demand and of how many sales associates are available on site. Yet, we already found a metric that describes traffic and staffing—Service Intensity. In Figure 5-4, Rachel's performance is in context to the Service Intensity levels in the Hello Store.

Figure 5-4 Rachel's Sales per hour—by Service Intensity

Outside	$233	$259	$253	$251	$250
Service	$251	$225	$231	$232	$230
Intensity	$231	$230	$244	$241	$254
	$237	$236	$251	$242	$245
	$238	$246	$254	$248	$250
	$256	$248	$257	$256	$266
	$261	$254	$277	$256	$278
With	$261	$256	$278	$256	$250
Service	$262	$266	$279	$262	$257
Intensity	$264	$266	$278	$268	$257
	$271	$268	$282	$273	$259
	$272	$270	$284	$276	$260
	$275	$273	$285	$285	$262
	$289	$278	$287	$287	$271
	$291	$284	$290	$291	$272

In the next phase of our journey towards an optimized schedule connects the measurement of store productivity and the metric of employee productivity.

THE PROBABILITY OF INDIVIDUAL PERFORMANCE

Service Productivity is the probability of individual performance, which is a function of the specific salesperson, and store operations. To predict future performance, we will deploy the statistics of Bayes' Theorem. Named after Thomas Bayes (1701-1761), the formula calculates a probability of an event based on knowledge of previous behaviors. The Service Productivity of an employee, therefore, is a function of the employee's baseline sales performance, performance when the store adhered to the Service Intensity ratio, and performance when the store operated outside the guidelines of the Customer Service Model.

For simplicity sake, we will focus on our chosen associate Rachel. Back at corporate, the manager of Workforce Management wants to forecast how much sales Rachel will generate regardless of the conditions in the Hello Store, including; shortage in staff; storms and heat waves; big sale of the season; or even construction in the shopping mall.

Figure 5-5 displays the process of predicting Rachel's productivity by combining our knowledge of her past Sales per Hour baseline and Hello Store's Service Intensity parameters.

Figure 5-5 Rachel's Probability of Performance

Step 1—Probability of Baseline Performance:

As we saw in Figure 5-4, out of 75 working days, Rachel's Average of Sales per Hour is $261, and the standard deviation is $17. Therefore, Rachel's baseline is $244 to $278 Sales per Hour. Rachel achieved her baseline levels in 52 out of the 75 days. Thus, the probability Rachel performs to her baseline is 69% (52/75=69%)

We can adapt the calculation to also include those days where Rachel exceeded her quota. However, the objective of baseline performance is to negate the influence of other variables, such as higher demand. Since the impacts of demand and operation are included in the next steps, we should limit the baseline performance to the ability of the individual salesperson. Remember the rule of thumb for management—a more accurate forecast generates more optimized operations, and profitability.

Step 2—Probability of Performance while the Store operates within Service Intensity:

Out of the 75 days, the Hello Store operated within the guidelines of the Service Intensity policy of a 3 to 4 ratio, for 60 days (Figure 5-3). During those 60 days, Rachel performed within her baseline for 44 days. As long as Hello Store operates within the Customer Service Model—where Service Intensity ratio is 3 to 4—then Rachel will perform within her baseline 73% of the time (44/60=73%).

Imagine a store you love to shop. It is never too full or too empty, the sales people are informed, and pleasant, and you are keen on the brand.

In such a store, salespeople tend to perform consistently. This has many benefits. One challenge faced by many retailers is how to compensate the associates. Using commission based selling has many disadvantages, including predatory sales tactics that tend to backfire. Creating a compensation structure that adheres to a consistent environment, has many benefits, including empowerment and stability for the employees, and profitability for the retailer.

Step 3—Probability of Performance while the Store operates outside Service Intensity:

Out of the 15 days the Hello Store operated outside the Service Intensity, Rachel achieved her Sales per Hour range of $244 to $278 in 7 days. Based on past performance, the probability that Rachel will achieve her baseline, despite the abnormal conditions in the store, is 47% (7/15=47%)

At first glance, retailers may feel that we have a problem only when the Service Intensity is too high, meaning we cannot serve customers according to our policy. However, a too low Service Intensity is also not good policy. The underlying objective is profitability—we want to avoid situations where we have "too many employees".

Step 4—Service Productivity (Probability of Future Performance):

Building a forecast for Hello starts with the Service Productivity of each employee. For Rachel, in Step 1 we calculated her past performance *regardless* of the conditions in Hello. Step 2 measures how Rachel functioned when the store operated in the parameters of the Customer Service Model. Step 3 formulates how Rachel performed when the environment did not adhere to ideal conditions. Finally, to predict Rachel's performance, we employ Bayes Theorem in Step 4 (Figure 5-6).

Service Productivity is the probability that, for a given level of traffic and service policy, the sales associate will repeat or improve past performance. It means that if we schedule Rachel in the Hello Store, in 78 out of 100 working days, she will probably generate sales in the range of $244 to $278.

Figure 5-6 Rachel's Service Productivity

Rachel's Baseline Performance		
Step 1: Probability of Baseline Performance	x	69%
Hello Store's Service Intensity Performance		
Step 2: Probability of Baseline Performance when the store operates within CSM Service Intensity	y	73%
Step 3: Probability of Baseline Performance when the store operates outside CSM Service Intensity	z	47%
Rachel's Service Productivity		
Step 4: Service Productivity (Bayes Theorem)	$xy/(xy+z(1-x))$	78%

Part of the story of optimization is the continual measuring and monitoring of staff performance. The more data we have, the narrower we can pinpoint the Sales per Hour band. In addition, once we identify top performers, we can build upon that information to train and improve other sales associates. In the long term, the objective is not only an accurate range of performance but also to increase the performance of all employees.

THE OPTIMIZED MARGINAL VALUE OF AN ASSOCIATE

Behavior Analytics in its purest form is the story telling of data. The best "Once upon a Time" stories have happy endings. Our story of schedule to demand ends when we build a model that optimizes the schedule based on both the store, and the employees. So let's play—"What If".

What if the store has 5 sales associates during the full two hours? As we saw, Mike started his shift at 12:30pm, at the height of peak demand period. Instead, let's assume Mike starts his shift at 11am and is working at his baseline performance of average Sales per Hour of $198 (See Figure 5-7).

Figure 5-7 "What If" scenarios with 5 Employees

11:00 to 12:00 - 5 Associates				12:00 to 13:00 - 5 Associates			
Staff	Trans-actions	$ Sales per Hour	$ Average Sale	Staff	Trans-actions	$ Sales per Hour	$ Average Sale
Abby	4	$248	$62	Abby	5	$303	$61
Bob	3	$223	$74	Bob	3	$201	$67
Jane	2	$321	$161	Jane	3	$296	$99
Mike	3	$198	$66	Mike	3	$198	$66
Rachel	3	$291	$97	Rachel	3	$276	$92
Totals	15	$1,281	$85	Totals	17	$1,274	$75
Hourly Traffic			48	Hourly Traffic			72
Hourly Conversion Rate			31%	Hourly Conversion Rate			24%

By adding Mike to the schedule, the Hello Store generates $1,281 (Figure 5-7), instead of $1,083, in the first hour (Figure 5-1), and $1,274 instead of $1,157, in the second hour. Assuming Mike's costs are $25 per hour (all-inclusive payroll hour), operating margin for the first hour is $173 ($1,281-1,083-$25=$173), and for the second hour it is $104.50 ($1,274-$1,157-$12.50=$92). In this case, adding the fifth employee during the first hour and for the first half of the second hour generated positive operation margins.

Taking everything together, we can start putting together the value of adding a sales associate, and optimize the schedule. The objective is to reach a point where the operating margin is zero.

Figure 5-8 Marginal Value of a Sales Associate

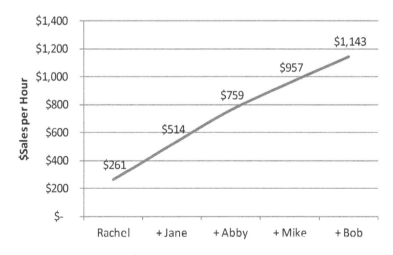

Figure 5-8 displays the Marginal Value of our five sales associates in Hello Store. The optimized schedule will add employees as long as the operating margin is positive.

A word of warning—the one direct result of this process tends to be that retailers schedule their best associates during peak hours. While the policy makes sense as in "put our top performers at the peak demand period", it can backfire. At low traffic periods, newer employees do not get the chance to improve their sales skills, and those who do not perform as well, can develop bitterness that lowers performance. Focusing on high earners instead of improving all employees is short-sighted. Moreover, the notion that lower prices can bring in more customers and differentiate a retailer, can last only for so long. Employees matter—more investment will bring better results.

In Schedule to Demand, Service Productivity provides the means and tools to measure, monitor, and predict performance of each individual employee. But the analytical and budgeting process should be taken in context with a training program, and as part of a corporate strategy and the local store guidelines, as defined by the Customer Service Model.

KEY POINTS
- In Schedule to Demand, Service Intensity monitors the performance of the physical store and Service Productivity is the metric of productivity for each sales associate.
- Service Productivity is the probability that, for a given level of traffic and service policy, the salesperson will repeat past sales performance.
- In an optimized schedule, we identify the balance between sales conversion and productivity.
- Service Productivity is the probability of individual performance, as a function of the specific salesperson and store operations, and is calculated with the statistics of Bayes' Theorem.
- Service Productivity can also serve as the basis for estimating the marginal value of a sales associate, by individual employees.

CHAPTER 6
BROWSING BEHAVIOR

My introduction to in-store analytics was in the middle of a tornado. I was flying to South Florida on a late Thursday night, and once we landed the captain announced that due to a tornado warning the airport had ceased outdoor operations. We stayed in the airplane, on the tarmac, about a mile away from the terminal, for an hour. To avoid thinking about the wind swirling outside and ignoring the uneasiness from how the plane kept shaking and slightly spinning, my seat-neighbor and I engaged in a conversion about work. I talked about traffic behaviors. He explained marketing techniques. We learned that traffic and marketing analytics are natural complements, and these disciplines present the core principles for in-store behavior metrics.

When retailers speak of in-store analytics in context of people counting, the conversation refers to measuring how many and for how long customers stay in a specific zone such as the lucrative spots in the end-of-the aisle (End-Caps), how long they loiter watching digital displays with advertising contents, or full-store tracking. Most of the business objectives relate to the product positioning in order to identify which aisle, which shelf, or how far from the coveted eye-level height, we should put the merchandize to maximize sales. Meanwhile, retailers learned about the many advantages of capturing each click and webpage view activities of customers online. In-store analytics aspires to mimic the online world for the physical site. Individual privacy challenges aside, the data trove from tracking employees and customers in the store can provide information to all the departments in a retail organization, from marketing to merchandising and finance.

In Schedule to Demand, the Customer Service Model metrics are geared toward store productivity by connecting traffic, workforce and point-of-sale systems. In Zone Monitoring, we define staying versus passing behaviors. In a department, we measure the sales conversion. In queue management we monitor customer service. For full store tracking, we monitor customer flow for the benefits of layout design and marketing. In short, in-store analytics pertain to customers and staff activities in zones, departments and sections, and how measuring, monitoring and predicting behaviors embed in the fabric of store operations.

Browsing Versus Buying Behaviors

Retailers have an overwhelming amount of data on buying behaviors. The point-of-sale systems spit out an incredible amount of details, itemized merchandize sold, array of transactions by period of time and type, and a slew of minutia on individual customers. As the primary consumer of sales data, the Marketing department targets buying behaviors for the purpose of increasing the basket size (more items per transaction) and increasing the shopping frequency (new and returned visits).

Sales data, however, provides insights into what customers actually bought. This "after the fact" data misses the whole spectrum of what happens during the visit in the bricks-and-mortar store. This is where "browsing behaviors" such as monitoring where the customers are, how long they stay in a specific area, and measuring interactions with employees. Browsing behaviors, therefore, aim to identify how the activities impact sales. This is the uncharted territory of in-store Behavior Analytics.

So far, most of the data on the store operations and activities come from customer surveys and mystery shoppers. As a result, a relatively small percentage of biased impressions, in a limited and selective period of time, serve as the foundation set of data for assessing store performance.

For example, a mystery shopper named Mary visited the store on Monday and gave it an excellent score of 90%. On Tuesday, a second mystery shopper named Betsy gave the same store a score of 70%. These scores do not show that by comparison, Monday had more traffic and lower conversion than Tuesday. Mary was fortunate to be helped by the store manager, while Betsy asked a question from a sales associate, who happened to start two days ago and had no idea where to find the suits on sale. Moreover, Mary found a great shirt for her son's birthday party; Betsy could not find pants that fit her properly. The scores are missing the context of what happened.

At the same time, 3 out of the 373 visiting customers on Monday filled out the customer survey with glowing recommendations of 9 and 10 out of 10. On Tuesday only 1 customer filled out the survey and the score was 8 out of 10. There were 491 visitors to the store that Tuesday. Best practices in customer surveys is the highest score of 10, with 1 being the lowest, indicate customers who voted 10 will recommend the retailer to their friends. That is great data from a marketing perspective, since it identifies customers who are considered as "influential", however, the statistical nature of the samples, while pointing to the best and worst situations, hinders consistent subjectivity.

In short, relying on mystery shoppers and customer surveys as a standard for store performance can be misleading. Combing data from traffic sensors (with the caveats of accuracy and cost), with sales, inventory tracking and workforce systems, generates additional insights into customers and staff activities. Counting technologies and applications can provide retailers with a more scientific way to measure and monitor the shopping experience.

Customer Behaviors

Great customer experience should translate into higher sales, however, as we see throughout this book, part of the challenge starts with how we define the comparisons. Comparing year-over-year sales results (Comp Sales) is a great indicator for the overall success, or failure, of the store. Much like the Gross Domestic Product (GDP) that provides an overall guide to the state of the economy, but will not indicate if the trends are caused by unemployment, housing shortage or trade surplus; we require more metrics to measure the shopping experience.

Below are some suggestions for measuring activities:

Occupancy Rate: The occupancy rate indicates the relative traffic to specific areas in the store of the total traffic in the store. For example: sections (i.e. pharmacy or office supplies); departments (i.e. women or petite); and aisle (i.e. wine or bread).

Currently, most projects of in-store analytics with traffic relate to designing new concept stores or monitoring customer flow in the flagship store. To minimize costs, instead of covering the full store, we can divide the store into sections.

The typical department store, for example, has about 10 to 16 departments, but can be divided into four or six big areas. Traffic counters along the virtual dividing lines can measure flow between the sections, and calculate the relative occupancy per period of time. For example, we can calculate that in the morning only 10% of visitors to the store spend time in the active apparel section, but 17% in the late afternoon. This makes sense if the store is located in an urban area where customers tend to shop for gym and yoga cloths after work.

Current technologies provide heat maps as a visual representation of the customer flow. Heat maps indicate where people congregate more (typically displayed in red) or less (white areas point to no traffic), and generate a picture of real-time customer flow and occupancy rate. Full-coverage of the store by video technology, however, is very expensive and is recommended for a test store where the detailed analysis of customer motion and employees' interactions can be performed or where the technology can also be utilized for other purposes such as loss prevention. The trend is moving toward the much less costly wireless technologies, which substitute accuracy with a statically valid sample of staff and customer behaviors.

Opportunity Rate: The number of visitors, and hence potential buyers, to a specific area inside the store. From a marketing perspective, the Opportunity Rate measures how many customers are in a specific location or engaging with a particular display. In Zone Management, the Opportunity Rate measures the number of customers in the zone.

The Opportunity Rate is a particularly effective metrics for Marketing. For example, monitoring the effectiveness of in-store marketing as it relates to the customers interaction with fixed and digital displays, how many customers stay in promotional areas such as a dais displaying the "hot items", and how signs affect the customer flow throughout the store. Another facet of Zone Management refers to brand management, in the sense of monitoring changes in traffic levels in a specific aisle or area once the retailer changes the marketing message.

Category Management pertains to customer engagement with a specific category of goods such as soft drinks, or individual products such as Coca-Cola. An interesting study in marketing indicates if there is a connection between two or more products, for example—do sales of Coca-Cola increase if the bottles are located in the deli section, next to the oven-baked chicken.

Shopping Unit: When two or more people have a unified purchasing power, they are considered as a Shopping Unit. Common examples are a mother and child in a supermarket or couples buying a television. The differentiation between a customer buying as an individual or as a part of shopping group has many implications on customer service, from sales training to how many cashiers are required at the checkout counter.

Some digital displays integrate facial recognition technology that can provide a sense of customer demographics such as gender, height, and color. While retailers have yet to deal with the privacy implications, vendors typically do not keep individual data but provide demographic information, by display, area, and the period of time.

Stay Time: Stay time reflects how long shoppers stay in a department, or a zone, and how long they engage with a particular display or fixture.

In Store Conversion Rate: The ratio between transactions and visitors (Opportunity Rate) in a particular location in the store, per period of time.

Due to their complexity, we will take a closer look at Staying Time and In-Store Conversion later.

Staff Behaviors

In addition to insights about customer activities, in-store behavior monitoring provides information in the performance of employees, specifically the visual monitoring of the staff's activities. Video analytics, while still evolving as the technology improves, can have many benefits. Such as—

Inventory: Much of the business benefit in tracking stocking activities relate to time studies. For example, how long does it takes an employee to stock a shelf, what is the best time for fulfillment, how often should employees check the shelves, and the accounting of Activity Based Costing. Traffic sensors add value by measuring stocking patterns in a consistent, real-time, manner.

Displays: Video technology also provides unbiased monitoring of displays, in the sense of ensuring that the branding concept is portrayed consistently, and according to corporate policy, in the stores.

Real-Time Deployment: Customer service metrics for in-store analytics include how to measure the interaction between customer and employee? How to measure productivity of the interaction? We discussed how to build the Customer Service Model using the metrics of Service Intensity and Service Productivity in previous chapters, and in chapter 8 we will address Predictive Scheduling.

Frontline Checkouts: Queue Management measures, monitors and predicts the behaviors of both customers and employees, and we will discuss this in detail in the next two chapters.

Abnormal Behaviors

Traffic monitoring also illuminates abnormal behaviors. While the selection of in-store technology—video, thermal or wireless—limits the nature of business benefit, some technologies can identify and react to behaviors the retailer considers as requiring investigation.

Loss Prevention: The most obvious application, especially for video technologies, is the dual-use deployment for traffic and loss prevention. While the nuances of the technology are relatively new and require more development, these applications can be divided into the following categories.

- **Monitoring Cashiers:** Identifying cashier activities, such as returns or opening the till, when there are no customers in the service zone.
- **Monitoring Displays:** Alerts managers when people loiter around fixed displays to prevent shoplifting opportunities.
- **Monitoring Objects**: Video technologies count by capturing the image of objects. If the object size changes "too much" but still moves, this may be a signal of hiding goods in cloths or bags.
- **Monitoring Exits:** Connecting between the Electronic Article Surveillance (EAS), which tags goods with radio wave tags to prevent shoplifting, and the traffic counters, to improve alerts.

STAYING VERSUS PASSING BEHAVIOR

Understanding in-store activities start with the definition of Opportunities—how many customers stayed long enough in a specific area to be considered as interested, and their staying time. Zone Management is the most common people counting solution inside the store, and it provides insights on passing versus staying behaviors.

Customer activities are of an interest to both the retailer and the brand manager. For example: Coke-Cola. In a supermarket we can find Coca-Cola in the soft drinks aisle, at the display counters next to the cashiers, and in the specialty deli area. With data from the point-of-sale system, the Coke Cola company would analyze which location generates more revenue, which bottle size sells, and if sales fare better if we switch the Coke with water bottles. By monitoring activities in the zone, we have information into how the customers interact with the product *before* the actual buying. We will also know how many customers *did not* reach out and put the Coke Cola bottle in their cart.

Define Zone Management

Zone Management is a people counting concept that emanated from the sensor's range of coverage. While each sensor's Field-of-View depends on the technology and lens, the assumption behind zone monitoring, is that it relates to a single sensor. This is important because of accuracy.

It is easier to develop, install, calibrate and verify the accuracy of motion within a single sensor, in comparison to tracking the movements of the same customer between two or more sensors. With the exception of wireless providers, when most companies discuss in-store analytics they point to the "viewing" capabilities of dual-use video or to the metrics of zone management.

The Yellow Store, for example, is a "Big Box" store that mostly sells general merchandise, with a newly minted electronics department, and about 30 employees on the sales floor. Yellow Store wanted to measure and monitor activities in the electronics department, specifically customer behaviors in and around the televisions and computers. Therefore, traffic sensors monitored and measured the area in front of the television wall display and the zone surrounding the tables displaying computers.

Defining Zone Opportunities

Not all counting technologies empirically count the number of people entering the zone; therefore it is imperative for the retailer to understand how the vendor measures the number of people inside the area. Some technologies can only define if the zone is occupied or empty; this means it does not matter how many people are in the zone since the output will always be either zero or one. Quality sensors track how many people enter and exit the zone, per period of time. Advanced counters can also identify group behavior in order to produce a count of Shopping Units (one or more people acting as a single buying group).

In areas where customers and employees typically stand, or sit, on either side of a display case or a table, it will be easier to exclude the employees from the count. For Yellow Store, we will assume the technology accurately measures the number of customers in the zone. In this case, the process of defining Opportunities is similar to the methodology of defining traffic to the store, hence—Demand.

In Figure 6-1, the data from the two display areas provides immediate clarifications. On Saturday, the hourly averages were 100 people in the television area and 50 people in the computers zone.

Figure 6-1 Customers and Staying Time by Zone

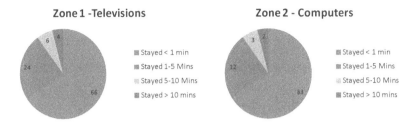

The in-store Customer Service Model should define the following—

* Is the Opportunity Rate what we expected, and why?
* Is there a difference between the Opportunity Rates of the zones, and why?

Staying Time

Measuring the staying time accurately, again, is dependent on the quality of the capture technology. For our purposes, we will assume that the technology measures individual time.

Staying Time is a Key Performance Indicator for Zone Management, which is a product of both the actual time and its percentage out of all customer activities.

Yellow Store decided to divide the stay time into four categories.

* Staying less than 1 minute is considered "passing by" behavior.
* Staying between 1 to 5 minutes means that the display incited the customers to stop and look, but there was no strong interest that required attention from the employees beyond a greeting or a quick answer.
* Staying between 5 to 10 minutes means that the customers interacted with an employee and were actively browsing the electronics products.
* Staying longer than 10 minutes implies that the customer has the intent to buy.

Stay Ratio: Another way of looking at the data is to calculate the relative percentage of a particular stay time range in context of all customers. In the televisions zone, 10 out of 100 customers stayed longer than 5 minutes. In the computers zone, 5 out of 50 people stayed longer than 5 minutes. Hence in both zones, we had 10% of the customers staying longer than 5 minutes.

If, as Yellow Store did, we assume that a "Stay Time" of longer than 5 minutes indicates true interest by customers, then the objective becomes increasing the Stay Ratio.

Identifying the optimal "Stay Time" requires connecting between activities and transactions, and we already know such a metric—Sales Conversion.

IN-STORE SALES CONVERSION

If calculating Sales Conversion for the store has too many rules and exceptions, then in-store sales conversion is a lot more complicated, primarily because of the technology. Part of the story is the ability to differentiate between the pass and stay behaviors. One part is excluding the counting of employees. Another factor is the choice between deploying complicated, expensive and accurate technology and tracking only those customers who have active Wi-Fi or Bluetooth features.

Sales Conversion for a zone is a relatively simple affair since the zone is a limited area and we have the technology count opportunities to link the customers to transactions. Monitoring departments is another story. Measuring the department conversion rate is the Holy Grail for Big Box stores and department stores. The challenges include a combination of the costs of the technology required to cover the store; the identification of customers versus employees' behavior; measuring the correct transactions; and correlating the timing of the browsing to a transaction in the point-of sales.

Back to Yellow Store—we wanted to calculate the Sales Conversion rate for the Electronics and Toy departments. The formula for conversion rate of a specific area is similar to calculating sales conversion for the store, except for the following caveats:

% Sales Conversion (Area) = Transactions (Area)/ Visitors (Area)

Defining Demand

Demand is defined as the Opportunity Rate for a location inside the store. There are technology challenges for covering an area larger than the field-of-view of a single sensor, but the objective is to define the number of visitors to that area, per period of time.

Demand, therefore, can be measured from:

- **Measured Tracking:** Full coverage of the store measures the number of people entering and exiting the area. The advantage of full coverage is in the rich detail of activities. The disadvantages are the expense and the difficulties in differentiating employees from customers.
- **Measured Occupancy**: Some vendors provide accurate occupancy count by covering the area with sensors. This is a less expensive solution than full-tracking, with accurate counts.
- **Calculated Occupancy**: The most common solution includes traffic counters, along the virtual lines of the area, and the calculation of occupancy (see Sales Opportunities Chapter).
- **Sampled Opportunities:** Pertains to wireless technologies where we can accurately track the customers who have active wireless features. Since not all customers are counted, we can use audits and point-of-sale data to make assumptions and calculate demand.

Employee identification: As radio waves tags (RFID) become more sophisticated and are able to interact with the traffic solution, the counting accuracy will increase. If there are no technological solutions, then certain assumptions can be made to account for behavior. This must be clarified and discussed with the retailer.

Defining Transactions

For Yellow Store, we looked at one transaction for a single shopping unit. Department transactions, however, must be mined from the unit level (SKUs). Consider these examples.

- Sarah bought a television and cable for her laptop. The transaction, consisting of 2 items, will be treated as 1 transaction for the store's conversion calculation. Television is 1 transaction in the Television area, and the laptop cable is 1 transaction in the Computers conversion calculations. For the Electronics area, the 2 items will be combined as 1 transaction (1 shopping unit—Sarah)
- Mike bought a cable connecting a television and a computer. For sales conversion in a zone, the cable will be counted as 1 in Televisions and 1 in Computers. For the Electronics department, the cable is considered as 1 transaction.
- Joan and Joel bought 3 toys for their kids and a television. For the store level, the 4 items and 2 people are merged to 1 transaction. In toys, the 3 items are 1 transaction. In Electronics, the television is 1 transaction.

Transaction Timing: A technical challenge is linking the customer activities to the point-of-sale transaction. Here, the advantage goes to wireless technologies and analytical applications.

In summary, there are many options to define parameters and calculation of the sales conversion for an area. The key is consistency. Decide on a methodology and stay with it.

REAL-TIME DEPLOYMENT

Once the retailer established the optimized Customer Service Metrics, the question becomes how to improve the overall performance of the store. This is done by deploying employees to in-store areas that require special assistance or expertise, in real time.

While the technology of real-time applications moves fast, the business benefits of deployment are hardly defined. Below are highlights of the process based on our case study in the Yellow Store.

Customer Service Model: Yellow Store defined the objectives of the pilot based on the following:

- **What is the impact on the Stay Time?** Yellow Store is interested in the number of customers staying longer than the minimum "true interest" staying time of 5 minutes.
- **What is the impact on Stay Rate?** Yellow Store's objective is to increase the Stay Rate for customers staying longer than 5 minutes by at least 1%.
- **What is the impact on Service Intensity?** Both the television and the computers zone had a Service Intensity rate of 25, and Yellow Store wanted to identify an optimal rate for each zone.
- **What is the impact on the Average Basket?** Yellow Store measured to see if the number of sale associates had any impact on the average basket size, for each product.
- **What is the impact on Revenue?** Yellow Store measured the increase, or decrease, in revenue.
- **What is the impact on Profit?** The decision to add, or subtract, a sale associate depended first and foremost on profit. As a community friendly store, Yellow Store's policy is—as long as profit levels stay the same, the store will add associates in order to improve the employment levels and at the same time enhance the customer service.

Proof-of-Concept: Yellow Store tested the added value of a sale associate based on the parameters:

- Add 1 associate to television
- Add 1 associate to laptops
- Reduce 1 associate to television
- Reduce 1 associate to laptops
- Move 1 associate from television to laptops
- Move 1 associate from laptops to television

Each of the above phases was tested on the same day (i.e. Tuesday), in the same period of time (i.e. late afternoon), within the same month, and all parameters are relative to the beginning baseline.

For retailers, a word of advice—treat the in-store analytics projects as economics experiments by keeping all variables but one the same until there is a "good enough" answer of the optimal traffic and staying time levels. My recommendation is to perform conceptual tests in at least 10 stores before committing to a corporate policy of scheduling. This is a data intensive project so prepare for a headache . . . Retailers who are continuously managing to data are leaders in their markets.

In-store behavior analytics is still nascent in the sense there are no serious complete roll-outs in the field. Much of what we discussed in this chapter is a combination of pilots and "wish lists"; however, the desire for information by retailers and rapid improvements in technology make it a promising area of discovery, and sales.

KEY POINTS

- In-store analytics pertain to customers and staff activities in zones, departments and sections, and how measuring, monitoring and predicting behaviors embed in store operations.
- Occupancy Rate indicates the relative traffic to specific areas in the store, such as departments and aisles, out of the total traffic to the store.
- Opportunity Rate is the number of visitors, and hence potential buyers, to a specific area.
- Stay time reflects how long shoppers stay in a department, or a zone, and how long they engage with a particular display or fixture.
- In Store Sales Conversion is the ratio between transactions and visitors (Opportunity Rate) in a particular location in the store, per period of time.
- Demand can be defined from Measured Tracking, Measured Occupancy, Calculated Occupancy, or Sampled Opportunities.

CHAPTER 7
QUEUE MANAGEMENT

Ask a retailer which is a better investment—a handheld point-of-sale or mobile device, or a queue sensor, and the most likely answer is the mobile device. The reason is simple. A mobile device is an action tool that speeds and adds convenience to the checkout process. A queue management system is passive, just measuring, monitoring, and predicting queue behavior.

"I can always see if there's a queue or not, why do I need technology?" I had heard this statement from so many store managers and corporate officers that it became a cliché. With all due respect to the store manager's self-confidence, retailers cannot run a business, especially not a multi-million corporation, trusting customer service on the premise that someone will take a peak. If queues seem unimportant today, they may be mission-critical tomorrow as the competition becomes fiercer and superior customer service becomes a potent advantage.

Queue Management systems monitor queue behavior in real-time, and provide data on how many people are standing in the queue per period of time, and for how long. Queue management is a term also used by vendors to describe technologies such as call-forwarding and self-service kiosks, as well as tools for customer flow, such as rail stanchions and displays, but, in the context of Schedule to Demand, the term Queue Management refers to non-intrusive, always on, measurement of queue length and waiting times.

The business objectives are to measure under-staffing or over-staffing to target, as defined by the Customer Service Model, as well as real-time measuring and monitoring of staff and customer activities. Thus predicting how many open cashiers are required in order to prevent the formation of queues.

Since the checkout is the last touch point before a customer leaves the store, the flavor of a dreadful incident at the end tends to tint the whole shopping experience. Queues take a variety of formats, from the simple line, to hubs in each department, and to the multifaceted frontline banks. Since queues, with more or less self-service kiosks or handheld cashiers, will not soon disappear from the bricks-and-mortar stores, and, since the frontline payroll is a considerable portion of costs in any retailer store, it is worthwhile to explore not only how to optimize frontline operations, but also how to enhance customer service.

DEFINE QUEUE MANAGEMENT

Customer Service Models for Queue and Frontline Service Management (Bulk Cashier Blocks) are defined by the retailer's history, customer behavior trends, and the marginal value of adding one sales associate in context with the store's operational profitability.

Most retailers have yet to dip into queue management and therefore are just happy to know how many customers are waiting in line. Supermarkets and Big Box Stores, however, are actively testing and designing queue policies for the frontline checkouts. And due to an analytics culture based on time studies, Retail Banking and Quick Service Restaurants are also engaged in the quest to enhance their speed of service.

Below are some Customer Service Models:

One in Front: Also known as "1+1", "One in Front" is the prevalent frontline service model for the handful of supermarkets that had rolled-out queue management in a significant number of stores. It means in any given time, one customer is being served, and one customer waits in the queue.

To be effective, One in Front requires a queue solution that captures group behavior and therefore can accurately measure Shopping Units.

Five-Five Rule: Queuing policies of having no more than 5 customers in line, waiting no more than 5 minutes, originated in Retail Banking due to Take-a-Ticket, Call Forwarding, and the nascent non-intrusive Queue technologies, which both complement and compete with each other.

Serve 90% in less than 3 Minutes: If the Average Transaction lasts 180 seconds (3 minutes), this is a successful equivalent to "One in Front" model. By adding the Service Level Measurement (SLM), retailers measure how often each local store operates within the guidelines of the customer service policy

Serve 80% in less than 2.5 Minutes: Supermarkets that compete by customer service have upped the competitive bar with queuing technologies. While SLM of 80% may sound low, it is higher than the 50% implied by working only with Average Waiting Time.

Wait less than 1 minute: Effectively this model is the "No Queue" manifestation, since it implies an Average Transaction is around 60 seconds and no customers are waiting in line. This service policy typically leads to over-staffing because store managers would rather keep a cashier active than have any customers stand in line for any period of time.

No Queue: Retailers aspiring to a true No Queue policy are actively deploying handheld checkout devices. This policy makes sense for electronics and jewelry retailers where customer service is an integral part of the sales process and transactions consist of limited items, effectively taking out the stand alone checkout process. No Queue policies take on a different meaning in frontline and hubs formats, and we will discuss these implications in Predictive Scheduling (see Chapter 8).

Service Time: Service Time in this context is equivalent to the point-of-sales Transaction Time. While not a queue management policy, service time has profound implications on the formation of queues and choosing an optimized Customer Service Model.

For example, in Retail Banking, if the Average Transaction lasts 2 minutes, than with 2 cashiers it is likely a "Maximum Wait Time of 5 Minutes" makes sense. Supermarkets with Average Transaction Time of 3 minutes in a main bank, 1 minute in express cashiers, and 2 minutes in self-service kiosks, have to build different scheduling policies just to be consistent.

A word of caution—since Waiting Time and Service Time are influenced by dissimilar factors, *never* build a policy that combines both metrics. Customer Service Models such as "Checkout Service Time no longer than 90 Seconds" are simply wrong!

Customer Perceptions

While this book provides data-based metrics, we cannot escape the fact that Behavior Analytics includes, well, behavior. Therefore we must bow a bit to psychology and talk about perceptions. Queue Length and Queue Flow (speed) affect customers in different ways—

The decision to enter the queue: Queue Length affects the perception of how long would it take to receive service. Customers' decision to enter a specific queue is framed by a notion of a "crowd", the perception on how fast or slow a queue moves, and their tolerance for waiting.

How long is "too long" differs by industry. For American supermarkets, 3 is a crowd, but banks can have 5 waiting customers. In high-population urban centers, 10 customers per queue lane is a good bargain. And in airports, well, sometimes there is nothing to do but grumble . . .

The decision to stay in the queue: Queue Flow, rather the perception of how fast the queue moves, influences the customer decision to stay, once she picked a queue and stood in line. Much depends on the "cost of moving". In supermarkets, customers with carts full of stuff tend to stay in the same lane simply because it is physically harder to move. Imagine— you have already put your groceries on the belt and the customer in front of the cashier has started searching for coins. If you cannot feel the urge to move with the understanding that you are stuck and patience is your only weapon, then it is time go shopping with your kids.

Queue Classifications

Queues can be classified into three key categories, Linear, Parallel and Unstructured. Also, due to the prevalence of frontline checkouts, we will address the different formats of Main Bank, Double-Deck, Duplex and Hubs.

Linear Queue: Linear queues, lines with an entry and an exit are "First In—First Out" behavior, and the most common queues. These queues can be found in almost any retail format, from specialty stores, to the main banks, in supermarkets and department stores, or bank branches. While queue structure may be similar, the tolerance levels for waiting influences how customers react to queues, and how retailers manage the checkout process. We will see examples in later chapters.

As we see in Figure 7-1, the advantage of linear queues is that customers exit the queue to the first available cashier. This speeds up the queue since customers requiring longer and shorter service time than the average tend to cancel each other. As a result, the Queue Flow depends mostly on the number of active tills and the average service time.

While retailers put a great deal of thought, and money, in managing the waiting experience with Call Forwarding to speed the exit from the queue, stanchions for customer flow, display cases for impulse buying, and digital messaging for in-store marketing, only the non-intrusive, and real-time, monitoring of the queue connects between workforce and customer service policies.

Parallel Queues: Parallel queues are multiple linear queues that run in parallel to each other. The linear line can be addressed by itself, but a Queue Management policy for parallel lines requires context of all queues together. One facet in defining parallel queues is the "cost of moving". We can see the "cost of moving" behaviors in supermarkets, where the customers pushing shopping carts tend to stay in the first lane they enter (Figure 7-2). Parallel lines are also common in airports and other establishments where there are multiple service stations and there is either not enough space to design a long linear queue or a lack of organizational energy to think more creatively about queues.

One advantage of parallel queues is order, which means once customers are in a specific queue they are "locked" in. This works well where customer service is secondary, for example in security areas of airports. The challenge is that the queue speed depends on the productivity of a specific service agent and the speed of service for each of the customers in front. Say you are standing in passport control and the person in front of you has forgotten to renew his passport, unfortunately you cannot move to another line, which means you will probably get stuck waiting for a while.

Unstructured Queue: Unstructured Queues, also known as Cloud Queues, refer to a virtual area where people congregated around a focal point as they wait for service.

The defining aspect of an unstructured queue is the loose form. Customers surround the service stations and the cloud queue evolves naturally within a virtual area.

Unstructured queues typically exist around self-service kiosks, containing 1 or 2 people, and rarely exceed 7 waiting customers.

Monitoring even the smaller unstructured queues makes sense if we look at the waiting experience as a whole and the self-service kiosks are part of the service mix. A word of caution—how long the person stands in front of the kiosk is not always similar enough to transaction time, especially if the service requires personal information. Searching for driver licenses among five suitcases can last a while and therefore bias the reported service time.

Figure 7-1 Linear Queue

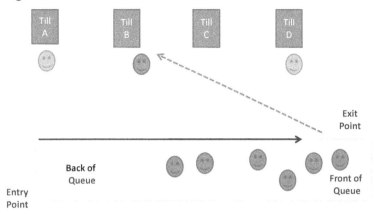

Figure 7-2 Parallel Queues

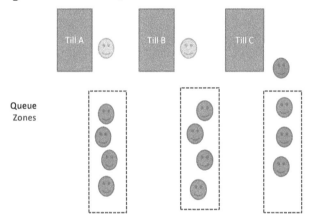

Figure 7-3 Unstructured "Cloud" Queue

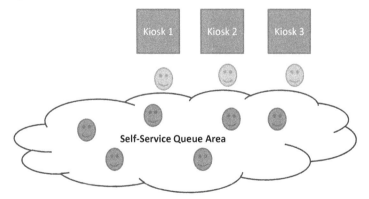

Frontline Service Management: In the context of Schedule to Demand, the Frontline relates to the checkout cashiers. The checkouts can be at the front of the store, as well as inside or in the back of the store, but for the sake of consistency, we will employ the term Frontline to any checkout dais, platform, counter, or bank, which carries a point-of-sale system and where the employees process transactions.

Frontline checkouts can include parallel, linear and unstructured queues. In supermarkets, main bank and express lanes are parallel, service desks have linear lanes, and self-service kiosks form unstructured queues. The main bank, however, has different formats that affect the nature of the queue and influence the process of optimization.

- **Main Bank:** Inclusive idiom for tills (cashier stations) that are situated one next to each other.
- **Double-Deck:** Tills with Front Cashier and Back Cashier stations, found in some department or Big Box stores such as Target. Double-Deck banks are a more efficient way to stack stations, and they work well as long as the queue length is short.
- **Duplex:** Tills with Left Station and Right Station, common to airports and cinemas. Here the queue exists per station, or as a single queue for both stations.
- **Hubs**: Spread out cashier stations. Checkout hubs can be located by department, and situated around the store. Hub format can also a bit deceptive as in Home Depot, where there is a group of cashiers in the main area and a group of cashier for the contractors section.

Queue Behaviors

Currently only a handful of companies have the capability for queue technology, and those who do so accurately are numbered by fewer than the fingers on one hand. Regardless of the technology, the solution must be able to detect, capture, and account for a variety of behaviors.

Group Behavior: For frontline service management, rather than focus on the number of customers waiting in line, retailers are focused on Shopping Units. This makes sense since the decision to open a till or not, depends less whether the checkout includes one or two or more people and more on the number and length of the transaction.

Group Behavior is captured by positioning—how two or more people relate to each other by Distance and Time (Figure 7-4)

Figure 7-4 Group Behavior

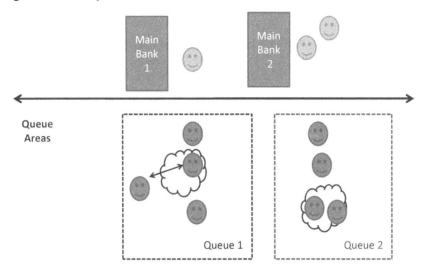

Since monitoring of group behaviors must be done in real-time, the process must be sensitive, flexible, and robust, to adapt to a diverse environment of a store. The accuracy of Group Behavior is a key differentiator for the vendors.

Figure 7-5 In Transaction Positioning

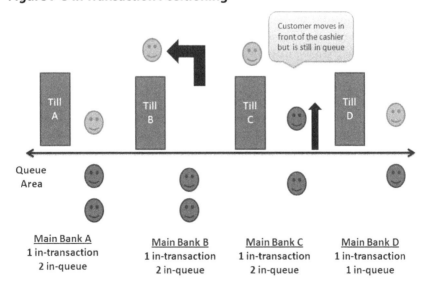

In-Transaction Behavior: Customers can move out of the service zone while the cashier continues to scan their shopping goods, and the transaction is still considered in-transaction (see Figure 7-5). This behavior is common in supermarkets where the basket contains many items and customers move forward, in front of the belt, and bag their merchandise. Since the service zone in front of the cashier is now vacant, the next customer can move forward despite still being considered part of the queue.

Vendors solve the in-transaction affect by monitoring the service zone and the belt for activity, or by connecting to the point-of-sale system in real-time.

Either way, the solution must account for this behavior. Customers stay part of the queue, until the in-transaction behavior resets.

Identify by Time: Discounting people who pass in and out of the zone without stopping is an important identifier, which impacts the consistency of accuracy. The technical definition of "passing" behavior depends on the direction of entry and exit, but especially on the staying time in the queue zone. For example, if people stay less than 5 seconds, than they are considered as "not in queue".

Identifying, and discounting, the people passing rather than those waiting in line is important for high-traffic stores where the checkout queues stretch into the aisle. In that case, the sensitivity of the technology to deal with the tight blend of passing and waiting behaviors is crucial. This is also where creative thinking into the store layout plays a role.

Identify by Direction: Identifying the direction of motion has many benefits for counting correctly. By defining "right" and "wrong" direction, we can discount people from the count, due to behavior. For example, the abandon rate from the queue is monitored by people exiting the queue from the wrong direction (not through the Queue Exit).

Another common feature for direction is used to identify employees in self service areas (Figure 7-6). Typically a desk is located at the exit point. The employee continuously enters and exits the service zone to help customers. An image that enters the zone from the exit point is labeled as "employee" and discounted from the number of customers in the zone.

Figure 7-6 Self-Service Behaviors

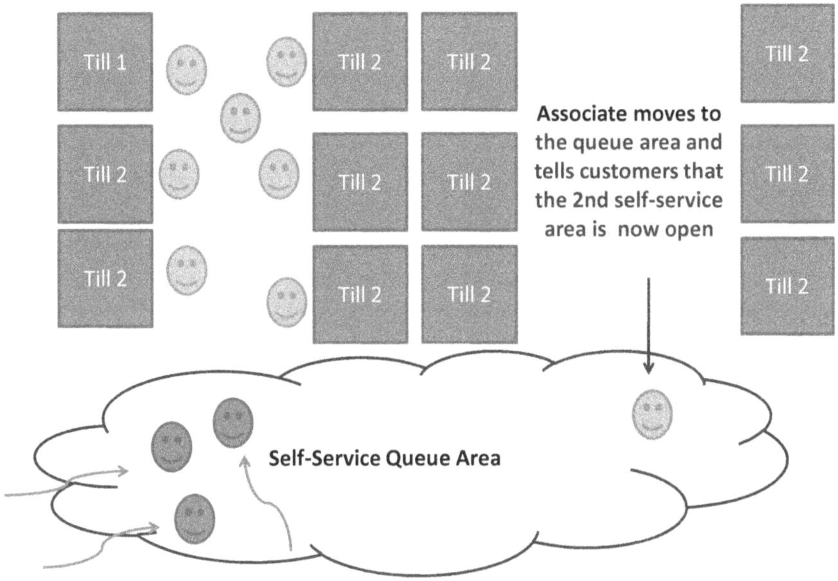

Associate moves to the queue area and tells customers that the 2nd self-service area is now open

Self-Service Queue Area

Identify by Location: Once we structured a virtual zone to denote a counting area, the accuracy of the counts can be improved by pinpointing the exact location of the image in the zone. Defining Back of Zone and Front of Zone helps in detecting loitering behavior, which can be seen beside the checkout in supermarkets, in the baggage claim areas in airports, or on waiting platform for trains.

Abandon Behavior: Abandon behavior is defined when a customer leaves the queue in the wrong direction. The natural behavior of people waiting in queues is forward; therefore if a person exits the queue either in the rear or to the side it is considered an abandon behavior. The technology that is directional in nature can easily distinguish abandon behavior.

In later chapters, we will discuss abandon behaviors in detail. To be accurate, the counting must be taken in context with the store environment and the type of retailer.

QUEUE COUNTING MODELS

Counting models for queue management measure and monitor how many people are waiting in line. Common models are "One in Front" or "Maximum Five in Queue" provide data on the minimum, average and maximum, per period of time, Queue Length.

Count-based models are common because they are easy to see, understand, explain, and therefore manage. Another reason is the technology. Counting is much easier to do than arriving at the waiting time correctly. For a detailed discussion on auditing, see the chapter on Accuracy.

The optimization process starts with building a baseline of behavior and identifying, per number of customers, how many lanes should be open, hence Target Lanes. Then we compare actual number of open lanes for the same number of customers, hence Actual Open Lanes. When we compare both, we can find the variance between optimal and actual active queues, calculate possible reductions in labor costs, and adapt the schedule to provide service according to the company's policy.

- **Over-Staffing:** When Target Lanes is higher than Actual Lanes, we open more cashiers to comply with the Customer Service Model.
- **Under-Staffing:** When Target Lanes is higher than Actual Lanes, we need to open more lanes to comply with the company's Customer Service Model.
- **Optimal Staff Levels**: The store functions according to the Customer Service Model.

Remember Big Foodie. The frontline area in our high-volume supermarket has 30 main bank tills, 5 express lanes, and 8 self-checkout kiosks. The following is the process of workforce optimization for the Customer Service Model of "One in Front", also known as "1+1".

In Figure 7-7, we see a day of data, per hour, of the following—
- **Actual Lanes**: Number of open lanes (per queue sensors)
- **Target Lanes:** Optimal number of open lanes based on "One in Front"
- **Average Queue Length**: Average waiting customers in all queues

Figure 7-7 Target Lanes vs. Actual Open Lanes

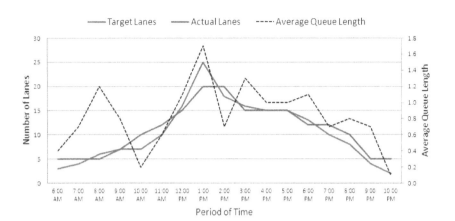

In our sample day, at 10am there were 10 open cashiers, and the system calculated a target rate of 7 cashiers. The Average Waiting value of 1.2 points to over-staffing because the metric is lower than Big Foodie Customer Service Model of 1 (One in Front).

By noon the lunch crowd rolled in, and by 1pm Big Foodie doubled the number of open stations from 10 to 20. Unfortunately, 20 active tills were not enough, as the average number of waiting customers shot up to 1.7 and the calculated Target Lanes was 25.

By 2pm, Big Foodie was still busy and kept the 20 cashier open, however the average queue length was 0.7 and the store only needed 18 tills to optimize frontline operations.

For simplicity, we assumed Big Foodie either opens or closes a lane for a full hour, which allows the metrics to be whole numbers. A word of caution—technology vendors calculate metrics differently, and retailers should understand the details and their implications.

Counting models require different models to be valuable in dissimilar queue formats and therefore are less effective when the retailer implements Predictive Scheduling.

WAITING TIME MODELS

Time-based models measure and monitor waiting times and provide the metrics for strategies such as "Serve Y% Customers in Less than X Minutes". Waiting Times policies are deployed regardless of the queue category (Linear, Parallel or Unstructured) or Frontline format (Main, Express, or Self-Service), which provide consistency to deploying associates in real-time.

Time-based models venture beyond the generalities of average and maximum queue length, into the details of the waiting behaviors using Service Level Measurement (SLM).

Back in our Big Foodie store, we wanted to identify an optimized queue waiting time. We took one period of time, say, the 4 to 5pm hour, where 15 cashiers were active, and counted the percentage of customers out of total customers waiting per each 15 or 30 second levels.

Figure 7-8 displays the results of the test—

- 96% of customers waited less than 180 seconds (3 minutes)
- 93% of customers waited less than 165 seconds
- 88% of customers waited less than 150 seconds (2.5 minutes)
- 82% of customers waited less than 135 seconds
- 79% of customers waited less than 120 seconds (2 minutes)
- 23% of customers waited less than 90 seconds (1.5 minutes)
- 17% of customers waited less than 60 seconds (1 minute)

Figure 7-8 SLM for Queue Waiting Time

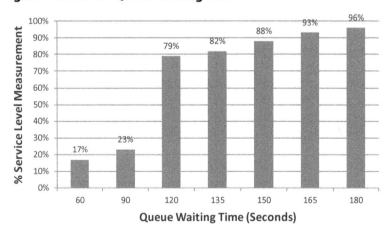

If the Customer Service Model was "Serving 95% of customers in less than 3 minutes", than the Big Foodie store functioned within policy parameters.

If Big Foodie desired the more competitive 2.5 minutes threshold, the Service Level Measurement was 88%. While 88% is respectable, if Big Foodie wanted to achieve 90% or even 95% of customers waiting less than 150 seconds, it needs to identify the process, and cost, of achieving this policy.

An interesting observation is the big drop in the number of customers waiting less than a minute and half. Considering Big Foodie is a high volume supermarket, where many people buy only a few items, where most transactions last between 90 to 120 seconds, the data makes sense. The customer who stands in queue less than 90 seconds is the first person in line. If we count only those situations where customers wait less than 90 seconds then, by default, there is only one customer waiting per queue.

Again, we offer a word of caution. Vendors have different ways of capturing and calculating waiting times, and retailers should clarify how, why, and what are the implications of the technology.

COUNTS VS. TIME MODELS

With a baseline of behaviors established, our Big Foodie store searched for an optimized Customer Service Model. The project was to identify the implications of the count models of "One in Front" versus the time-based model of "Serve 90% of customers in less than 3 minutes". In Figure 7-9, we see the differences between Counting and Time models.

Figure 7-9 Waiting, Wait Time—15 Minutes Segment

End Period	Queue 1 Waiting	Queue 2 Waiting	Queue 3 Waiting	Avg Queue Length	Queue 1 Average Time	Queue 2 Average Time	Queue 3 Average Time	Frontline Avg Wait Time	Active Cashiers
3:01	1	0	0	0.3	108	90	61	86	3
3:02	1	2	1	1.3	109	133	108	117	3
3:03	0	0	2	0.7	79	71	177	109	3
3:04	1	2	2	1.7	108	124	126	119	3
3:05	0	0	2	0.7	63	74	159	99	3
3:06	2	2	1	1.7	187	166	113	155	3
3:07	1	2	2	1.7	96	195	158	150	3
3:08	0	0	2	0.7	69	66	128	88	3
3:09	2	1	1	1.3	166	96	109	124	3
3:10	2	0	1	1.0	179	70	92	114	3
3:11	0	2	2	1.3	84	127	165	125	3
3:12	1	2	2	1.7	97	128	179	135	3
3:13	1	2	0	1.0	93	138	80	104	3
3:14	2	2	2	2.0	164	134	154	151	3
3:15	2	2	1	1.7	149	122	110	127	3

15 Minutes Summary			Avg Waiting	% SLM of '1 plus 1'	Avg Wait Time	% SLM T<2 min	% SLM T<2.5 min	% SLM T<3 min	Avg Open Cashiers
			1.2	73%	120	51%	73%	96%	3

Our sample consists of 15 minutes, in 1 minute increments, for 3 queues. The information includes the maximum number of customers waiting in each queue for each minute, and the average waiting time of those customers. We also calculated Average Queue Length and Average Waiting Time for the three queues (highlighted cells). Then we formulated the 15 minutes summary and the Service Level Measurement for the counts model of "1+1", and for the time-based models of the customers waiting less than 120, 150 and 180 seconds.

How we calculate the data would lead us to different conclusions—

Average Waiting: Calculating the average number of waiting customers for the 15 minute segment, we take the average queue length from 45 data points. To comply with a One in Front strategy, an Average Waiting value of 1.2 means the solution will require opening an additional lane.

SLM for "1+1": The success rate of each 1 minute, measured for the 15 minute segment, provided a Service Level Measurement of 73%. In other words, if the Customer Service Strategy was "1+1" than Foodie stood within the parameters of the policy for only 73 out of 100 customers.

Average Wait Time: Calculating the Average Wait Time from the 45 data points gives us 2 minutes. Contrary to the output from the Average Queue Length that required more lanes, the Average Wait Time results are a very competitive service policy. While this is a focused sample, the results tend to replicated in the field. In summary, *counting models tend to over-predict*.

A side effect of working with the imprecise counting models is the need for constant checking and resetting mechanisms, which are supported by real-time connections with the point-of-sale system. By monitoring when there are no transactions for a period of time, the system knows that the queue is empty, and the counter resets to zero. Unfortunately, real-time connectivity of both the traffic and point-of-sale is a technology nightmare. This is a key factor of failure for queuing projects. This also provides a competitive advantage to vendors who can, accurately, measure the waiting time.

SLM for 2.5 Minutes: Based on 45 data points, 73% of customers waited less than 2.5 minutes in the queue. If 73% sounds familiar, it should. This was the SLM for "One in Front". This means that we can make equivalent the strategies of "1+1" with "waiting less than 150 seconds".

Time-based models are the cutting edge techniques for workforce optimization. Customer Service Models take Wait Time in context with other productivity metrics such as Transaction Time and Idle Time, for a robust, data-analytics view of store operations.

Queue Management is exactly what it means—managing the queue. We do not estimate, we do not guess, we may use the frontline and handheld devices, but first we manage to a corporate Customer Service Model. How we work in the store, with Service Level Measurements (SLM), monitored in real-time, and predict how many cashiers should be open in order to react to forming lines and prevent queues, is the topic of the next chapter.

KEY POINTS
- Queue Management systems monitor queue behavior in real-time, and provide data on how many people are standing in the queue per period of time, and for how long.
- Customer Service Models for the queue include, One in Front (1+1), Five-Five Rule, Serve 90% in less than 3 Minutes, and No Queue.
- Queues can be classified into three key categories, Linear, Parallel and Unstructured.
- Frontline formats include Main Bank, Double-Deck, Duplex and Hubs.
- Group Behavior is captured by positioning—how two or more people relate to each other by Distance and Time.
- Customers need to stay part of the queue, until the in-transaction behavior resets.

- Counting models compare Target Lanes to the Actual Active Lanes, for Over-Staffing, Under-Staffing, and Optimal Staff Levels.
- Time-based models are the cutting edge techniques for workforce optimization. Customer Service Models take Wait Time in context with other productivity metrics such as Transaction Time and Idle Time, for a robust, data-analytics view of store operations.

CHAPTER 8
PREDICTIVE SCHEDULING

Predictive Scheduling is the real-time management of the bricks-and-mortar store by redeployment of available workforce resources. So far, Customer Service Models have dealt with the structuring of corporate policies and defining the Key Performance Indicators (KPI). Predictive Scheduling, in the context of Schedule to Demand, is the metrics and tools of what the store managers need to know, when, and what can they do to optimize profitability, operations and customer service.

Predictive Scheduling is a nascent technology, which presently only exists in the realm of Frontline Service Management, but it has the potential to change how we manage a bricks-and mortar store. In browsing behavior we offered metrics that paint a real-time picture of the store's activities. In Predictive Scheduling, our focus is on the only factor store managers can influence in real-time—where to position their employees where they matter the most.

DEFINE PREDICTIVE SCHEDULING

Predictive Scheduling defines the business benefits of deploying on-site labor resources; therefore, there are two key components required to make it work. The technology should be able to measure both customer and employee activities in real-time, and then accurately predict how to optimize the available resources to the Customer Service Model. In addition, the store must be able to react to actual demand; in other words, the store needs the capability to deploy the available resources. First we will define Predictive Scheduling.

Since Predictive Scheduling is today primarily a frontline application, we will focus on a method of predicting how many cashiers should be open now and in the next 5, 10, 15, or 30 minutes in order to prevent the formation of queues.

Frontline Service Management
A Predictive Scheduling solution monitors queue behaviors and demand trends; sometimes connects in real-time with point-of-sale and workforce systems; measures the number of customers waiting and for how long;

how many cashier tills are open or closed; analyzes basket size, shopping carts, and service time; and predicts how many cashiers should be active within a specific time frame.

Vendors have different capture technologies, analytics platforms, and management approaches to Predictive Scheduling, but there are two high-concept frameworks. The first method starts with demand at the door, which statistically estimates how many customers should end up in the main bank, express or self-service kiosks, and when. The second method originates with queue behavior, and adds data from the door, point-of-sale, and labor systems to enhance the prediction process.

There are distinct differences between the handful of vendors capable of Predictive Scheduling, and retailers should consider the implications of their chosen method, including installation, calibration, integration, and the accuracy rates.

Below are the key data feeds for the analytics of Predictive Scheduling:

Demand starts at the Door: The number of people entering the store starts the predictive process. The analytical solution estimates whether customers will end up in the main bank, express lanes, self-service kiosks, or walk out without buying. The challenges to an accurate forecast include how many customers are considered Shopping Units, and the correlation between historical trends to actual behaviors.

Stay Time: Stay Time, also known as Dwell Time, indicates how long customers stay in the store. The calculation of the total staying time in the store based solely on anonymous door-counting is exploratory at best. The full-tracking of individual customers is an expensive proposition. Wireless technologies are good with samples of behavior, not accuracy. Bottom line, Stay Time distributions from door to checkout are typically estimates based on historical trends.

Service Time: Service Time in this context is equivalent to Transaction Time, and refers to how long the customer stands in the service area, in front of the cashier, and receives services. A higher service time than usual will result in longer queues than planned, and test the predictive analysis.

Open or Closed Tills: Whether the service is the frontline in a supermarket, the checkout counter in a specialty store, teller services in a bank, or an immigration agent in the airport, the number of open service stations, and in which period of time, has a profound effect on the formation of queues.

Integration with Point-of-Sale: Real-time integration between traffic and point-of-sale systems enhances the prediction capability by comparing the data from the two solutions. It is also a cost savings measure since we can use Transaction Time and would not need a traffic sensor above the service area to monitor the Service Time. Real-time connectivity, however, is a technical nightmare. Regardless, batch upload of sales data every hour, 4 hours, or daily, are recommended since they improve the prediction process.

Integration with Workforce Management: Connecting traffic and schedule offers a complete view of the store, including how many stations are currently open, how many should be open in the next 5, 10 or 15 minutes (depending on the average stay time in the store), and which employees are on-site, their skills, and their availability.

By definition, Predictive Scheduling requires integration between traffic and workforce systems, but vendors are only starting to explore the connections between the technologies. At this point, workforce management and traffic management are two distinct markets that have yet to discover each other. Schedule to Demand, hopefully, will change this paradigm.

Fast forward five years into the future and imagine a dashboard where the store manager sees in real-time how the store operates, how many and where the customers are, and the system will suggest the most appropriate place to position the available employees. The role of Predictive Scheduling is to bring all the pieces of the puzzle into a feasible and effective framework.

Optimizing Idle Time: Optimizing productivity occurs when employees work to their maximized capacity without harming service. Idle Time refers to "dead" time periods where the station is active (employee is present) but there is no service activity.

While frontlines are typically managed to a slight over-capacity to ensure compliance with the customer service model, the objective is to avoid 'spikes' of Idle Time. For big retailers, reducing Idle Time by a couple of percentage points can translate into millions of dollars.

Real-Time Analytics

While Frontline Service Management dominates the applications for Predictive Scheduling, retailers and technology companies are actively working on predictive applications for more queue formats and for the browsing behaviors. All these analytical applications share the same form in the sense of comparing the actual queue behavior to the Customer Service Model.

To understand how Predictive Scheduling works, remember Little Foodie, our neighborhood store. Little Foodie has 3 tills, and the average transaction lasts 2 minutes, or 120 seconds. The store competes on customer service and is searching for the optimized frontline policy (Figure 8-1).

Figure 8-1 Queue Waiting Time

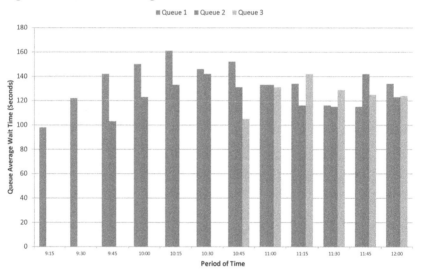

The key to comparing Customer Service Models to actual behavior is by understanding the reaction time. In Little Foodie, as long as the average waiting time in the queue is less than 120 seconds - which is comparable to the average transaction time of 120 seconds - the store effectively runs according to the policy of One in Front.

At 9:15am, Little Foodie opened one lane and at 98 seconds the waiting time stayed below the compliance threshold. Since the store keeps a strict policy of One in Front (equivalence to 2 minute wait time), any indication that there is more than 1 customer waiting in line requires action. By

9:30am, the waiting time of 122 seconds passed the threshold, which alerted the manager to open a second cashier by 9:45am.

With 2 stations active in the next three time periods, Little Foodie waiting times hovered above 120 seconds. The store manager did not feel that traffic in the store justified moving an employee from stocking activities to the frontline. By 10:30am it was obvious that 2 cashiers cannot comply with the maximum 2 minute wait time, and a third cashier opened.

From 10:45am onwards, with 3 active cashiers, Little Foodie had a 100% success rate of staying below the two and half minutes waiting time threshold. That said, 152 seconds wait time in a queue indicates that if the store had not opened the third lane so early, the store may have breached the 150 seconds threshold when demand increased toward lunchtime.

Predictive Scheduling must account for the maximum capacity, as we saw in Little Foodie with the 3 cashiers, and for behavior parameters that detect a swell in queue wait times and demand.

The long-term objective of implementing Predictive Scheduling is to see a consistent horizontal line close to the KPI threshold, i.e. 120 seconds.

REAL-TIME DEPLOYMENT

The other part of a successful real-time management requires the store to have information tools and be able to redeploy staff. This means the store manager must know what is going on, receive alerts to do something, and have the correct staff on hand in order to redeploy to actual demand. Analytics and Deployment are two conditions that go hand-in-hand, and one cannot exist without the other for Predictive Scheduling to be meaningful to store operations.

Predictive Dashboard

The Predictive Dashboard can be displayed on the store manager's computer, mounted on a wall, or presented as an application in a handheld device, have fancy graphics or a simplified green screen, but first retailers must define the business objectives. Once we have agreed upon the Customer Service Model and Key Performance Indicators, the dashboard also needs to address the following:

Define the Audience: Store managers, cashiers and corporate officers have different needs from the Predictive Dashboard, yet all require the same basic format—keep it simple, provide access for additional information, and quickly send alerts when action is needed.

A word of caution—some retailers and vendors are big proponents of customer displays. It has been my experience that customers (and the rest of us . . .) require simplicity. A digital monitor displaying the waiting time shapes the perceptions of customer service and is highly recommended, unless, of course, the wait time is absurd, such as a three hour wait in the airport . . . The Predictive Dashboard for operations is best kept within the confines of store personal.

Define Levels of Transparency: Most retailers limit the ability of an employee to access data to only the local store. Some companies allow, and even encourage, sharing data under the aegis that internal competition improves overall results and spreads best practices.

This is an interesting debate, with many implications from individual privacy to corporate theft and real-time deployment practices, and it will shape the future of Predictive Scheduling.

Define Deployment Priorities: Is not enough to define Customer Service Models, but we also must prioritize the relationships between the different models. In a Big Box specialty store, for example, the decision to move an employee from customer service in a department to the checkouts during a period of high-volume traffic may hinder sales conversion and basket size but increase service at the "last touch point".

A word of caution—defining in-store scheduling priorities is where most retailers fail in the process of communication between corporate and the local store. The danger lies in running disconnected projects without a comprehensive Customer Service Model, and where failure of input and feedback feeds can destroy a promising solution.

Passive versus Interactive Dashboard: Current technology of dashboards offers information, but the success to better predictability is continuous feedback on the prediction and actual activities. This is where the predictive applications are lacking, and where true innovation should happen.

The next step is to calibrate the format of alerts.

Define Alert Categories

Alerts are categorized by the number of customers, their stay time, and a relative percentage.

- **By Customers:** Structured by Opportunity Rate, for example, the system sends a warning alert when there are more than 5 customers in the television area, and an over-capacity alert, when there are more than 10 customers at the same time.
- **By Time:** Once the stay time reaches above 5 minutes, the "true interest" level, the associate is effectively "not available", and therefore requires backup.
- **By Percentage:** We can define the Stay Rate or Stay Time level as a percentage and alert the store manager if there is indication for a change. For example, we can use SLM. The system will send an alert if more than 10% of total customers in the last 15 minutes, waited longer than 2 minutes.

Define Alert Frequency

After we define the requirements for the alert categories, we need to establish when the alerts should be sent to the store manager.

- **By Period:** Managers may want to receive a status report at regular intervals, such as every hour, or every 4 hours.
- **By Threshold:** An alert is sent once the metric reaches a certain threshold, such as the stay time passes the 5 minute mark. There are many varieties of threshold, such as segments of time, levels, or a combination, which depend on the nature of the organization.
- **By Rolling Threshold**: The alert is sent when the threshold is held for a period of time, for example, the average stay time is longer than 5 minutes, for the past 10 minutes.

The Empowered Employee

No software program can replace the employee otherwise we would be buying all things on World Wide Web. For deployment policies to work, we should know not only what to do, but also what *can* we do. This is where employee skills, corporate policies, and aligning incentives come to play.

Multi-Tasking: Most retail employees are still tasked by simple activities such as move, sort, and stock goods. Some are trained to serve as cashiers. A few learn how to meet and greet, and what to do with an angry customer. This must change if the primary tasks are to become service and sales.

Retailers will need to do some soul searching. In a specialty Big Box such as a home improvement store, should the expert in hardware stay in the department to sell, or should he be deployed to the "last touch" point of the frontline? As the store becomes busier, the question is more vital. Smaller stores such as luxury retailers, need to ask what is more important, and when, to manage the store or serve a client? Such obvious dilemmas also exist in government. Should a Post Office worker sort mail or open another service station?

How many multi-skills employees are required on each shift, and what kind of skills are needed, is a key question during the proof-of-concept phase.

Floaters: Floaters are defined as employees scheduled not for a task, such as cashiers or working in a department, but as helpers where help is needed the most. Luckily for big stores, floaters may be a good solution for many scheduling challenges. For small stores with a limited number of employees, this question becomes moot and the focus should be on better scheduling.

Aligning Incentives to Policy: Predictive Scheduling is an information tool for the store manager, and will add value only if the employees trust the system and have the incentives to use the data. An under-staffed store, for example, will have difficulties sustaining quality service levels. An over-staffed store may challenge any reduction in scheduling. Compensation plans should adapt to a data-rich environment, where the theme is not just a fixed level of outcome, but continuous improvement.

Employees on the sales floor are not blessed with a long working life. High turnover, low pay, and a point of view that attributes labor to a cost center is how most executives view their employees. In a Schedule-to-Demand world, this frame of mind must change.

OPTIMIZED CUSTOMER SERVICE

Predictive Scheduling is the epitome of optimizing store operations and customer service. In a super competitive retail environment, where price shopping is a click away, customer service is no longer just a marketing cliché but an operational necessity.

In our 50 stores of the Special Chain, the checkout in all stores is a frontline, where customers wait in a linear queue that opens to a group of 8 to 16 stations, depending on the size of the store. For consistent comparison, regardless of the local conditions of the store, Special Chain employed the Queue Wait Time as the Key Performance Indicator.

In Figure 8-2, we compared each store's success rate, the Service Level Measurement (SLM), in achieving the coveted 2 minute waiting time, in context to the traffic volume (weekly visitors). In general, the average wait time was longer in stores with more traffic.

This inverse relationship of traffic and waiting time is similar to the correlation between traffic and sales conversion. In short, with more traffic and a lower service level, we are missing opportunities.

Figure 8-2 SLM for 2 Minutes Wait Time—Baseline

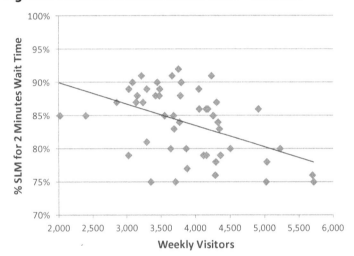

A year later, the same comparison generates much improved results (Figure 8-3). In the baseline, the success rate of the 2 Minute Wait Time Policy, while averaging at a decent 84%, ranged from 75% at the bottom, and varied across 17 points. After installing a queue management system and introducing predictive scheduling, the stores were able to adapt quicker to actual demand. If the Service Level Measurements (SLMs) in the beginning of the project were from 72% to 92%, than after a year the band tightened from 85% to 92%, with a higher average at 89%.

Figure 8-3 SLM for 2 Minutes Wait Time—Year 1

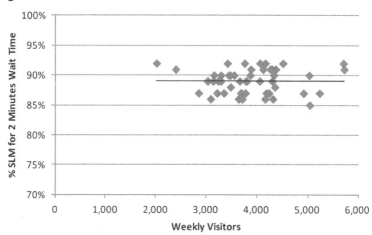

With well-managed frontlines, the average waiting line is linear, and horizontal; this points to rapid deployment as the queues form, and in particular, the effectiveness of predictive scheduling. We can also test the accuracy of the prediction against historical data for both validating and improving the solution. In summary, the "More Flat" Regression Line means that the store is less sensitive to changes in demand; the service level stays consistent regardless of the number of customers.

The trend of department stores selling groceries and supermarkets adding electronics and services to their stores, opens new avenues of using demand data for sales conversion and service intensity, but also it complicates the predictive process for the frontline.

Predictive Scheduling, in a way, is the Big Data application for managing retail stores, especially Big Box formats, and locations with a high-volume of people such as airports and train stations, and as a result, represents an opportunity for innovative technology and creative business thinking.

KEY POINTS
- Predictive Scheduling is real-time management of available workforce resources
- Predictive Scheduling currently is primarily a frontline application, measuring, monitoring and predicting how many cashiers should be open in order to prevent queue formations outside the parameters of the Customer Service Model.

- Minimizing Idle Time indicates optimizing productivity, which occurs when employees work to their maximized capacity without harming customer service.
- Predictive Scheduling needs to take into account the maximum capacity of the store, and the behavior parameters that detect a swell in queue wait times and demand.
- Analytics and Deployment are two conditions that go hand-in-hand, and one cannot exist without the other for Predictive Scheduling to be meaningful to store operations.
- For deployment policies to work, we should know not only what to do, but also what *can* we do. This is where skills, training and aligning incentives come to play
- With effective Predictive Scheduling, the level of service is less sensitive to demand; the service level stays consistent, regardless of the number of customers.

BOOK 2
Behavior Measurement

CHAPTER 9
TECHNOLOGY

The behavior measurement technology of Schedule to Demand is, at its heart, a "people counting" solution. The foundation for measuring people's activities is a Capture Technology such as infrared beams, thermal imaging, video analytics, and wireless systems. Since the form of the market and the who's who in vendors change as fast as these words are written, here we will only highlight the core characteristics of the technologies that translate images and waves into people's behavior.

Retailers often interact with Value Added Resellers (VARs). Resellers typically manage the project, provide the customer interface application, sometimes offer an analytics platform, and sometimes assist in the value development process. The advantage of resellers is they offer a "single point of contact". The disadvantage is resellers often mask the nature of the capture technology, and are not always knowledgeable enough to deal with the nuances of the minutia. A handful of companies are technology originators that sell directly to retailers, yet none can provide the best-of-breed in both capture technology and analytics. The objective of this section is to provide retailers with the basics of how this market works and what to ask the technology companies.

Presently the "people counting" market is attributed to traffic counters at the door, which means a sensor is mounted at the entrance to count how many people enter and exit the store. The trend is to push the sensors into the store itself, including monitoring in-store behavior and the checkout frontline area. The sensors can be simple and send a signal to an in-store computer or to a remote central server. They can also be smart devices, which both capture and analyze raw data. This reflects the shift to software where the competitive edge is in both capture and analytics technologies.

Behavior measurement solutions are judged by bandwidth, price packages, and ease of installation, calibration and maintenance. We will cover the formats of each solution in the next chapter. In addition, accuracy is the most defining feature of a solution, and we will dedicate a chapter to best practices in accuracy and auditing. Vendors are differentiated by their core technology and specific product, the structure of the data management platform, and the quality of support services.

For retailers, one of the secrets to success of a behavior analytics project is defining the Request for Proposal (RFP) in such a way that there are clear representations of the strengths and weakness of each aspect of the solution, and their impact on the Customer Service Model.

Analytics applications for retail are shifting from standalone, simplified reporting of traffic metrics, to a more inclusive platform of store operations, including loss prevention, supply chain, workforce and point-of-sale systems. Schedule to Demand presented the requirements for the technology and we will leave the quality of the analytics applications in the hands of the vendors themselves. In this chapter we will focus on technologies that capture people's behavior.

INFRARED BEAMS

Infrared beams are mounted either sideways on the door or top-down from the ceiling. These low-cost devices are simple to install and setup. The device sends a direct infrared beam, and counts the person moving across the doorway once the beam is broken.

The advantage of beam counters is their cost and simplicity. Unfortunately beam counters suffer from accuracy challenges. First, the sensors cannot recognize the direction of motion, and as a result, count both the people entering and the people leaving the store in a single bucket. This requires dividing the counts in half in order to estimate the number of people entering the store.

Secondly, in wide entrances or in high-traffic entrances, the system tends to undercount since it cannot differentiate between groups of people. If the beam is broken the system counts one, whether it is one person, or two or more people passing through the threshold. When customers loiter around the entrances or when shopping carts are within the beams range, the system cannot recognize the different behavior and over counts. Since the system can easily under-count and over-count, the inconsistencies may render the accuracy rate irrelevant.

Beam counters are best used as an alternative to no counters at all, or in-door situations where the motion is a straight forward walk with no displays or shopping carts close or in the pathway of the beam. For solutions where the quality of the data is important, it is better to avoid beam counters.

THERMAL IMAGING

Thermal imaging works by detecting emissions from moving targets, by locking on to the targets and then tracking them within the sensor's field of view. Thermal imaging ignores the background features and focuses only on the moving object. As a result the technology is not sensitive to light and allows the sensors to function well in challenging conditions such as fluctuations from darkness to bright light. Thermal also ignores the impact of shadows on the image.

While the accuracy can suffer from the 'blending' of a person's heat signature into their surroundings if the person stands too long in the same place, thermal imaging technologies achieve 95% or more accuracy rates in non-fluctuating ambient environments.

Thermal imaging based detectors are relatively easy to install and unless used for the sophisticated solutions such as queue management they are easy to calibrate. As low energy appliances, with no privacy issues since no image is taken, thermal sensors are versatile and wide spread.

VIDEO ANALYTICS

Video Analytics is the technology used to capture an image and analyze its content. The technology is based on identifying and tracking people activities, specifically motion detection; lines, borders or zone crossings; object recognition; and analytical metrics.

In people counting, Video Analytics technologies can be classified as a single monocular camera or as stereo vision with two cameras. The analytical engine can process the captured images either on an in-store server or on a smart device that is both a camera and a computer (At-the-Edge).

Single Lens Sensors

Monocular devices capture images through a single lens camera. The image can be processed within the sensor itself or sent to an in-store server or a smart unit for analysis. Due to costs and bandwidth requirements, the sensors typically send only metric data to the central server. For door-counting, monocular devices can achieve the coveted 95% accuracy in 90% of the stores. Since prices have plunged in the last couple of years, single lens devices are the most common capture technology.

The key challenge of monocular devices is their treatment of depth. In addition, monocular devices have great difficulty in measuring time correctly due to their inability to "hold on" to a specific image in rapidly changing motion and standing behaviors. The presence of shadows and changing ambient conditions during the day challenge the ability of the technology to compare the real-time image to a "baseline" picture.

The answer provided by many companies is to compare and "fix" the data to a trend, which happens during the daily upload to the central server, and even in real-time calculations. While traditional traffic application may have survived fixing the data for a gala event that tripled traffic, in Predictive Scheduling for queue management, the constant adjustment to the average queue length can create on-going errors and dilution of the data.

In summary, single lens devices can be accurate for most counting situations and due to the variety of vendors have, more or less, reached a commodity status.

Stereo Vision Devices

The accuracy of measuring behavior starts with capturing the most high-resolution image. This is best captured by a stereo vision camera that creates a three-dimensional view of the tracked object.

The four data points for each view—height, mass, speed and direction—significantly enhances the accuracy of the count. Since sunlight and shadows do not have depth, stereo vision devices can filter out these objects from the counts. This architecture also allows for individual tracking of the object, as well as the person or shopping cart, for an extended period of time. The ability to define the exact location of an individual person opens the door to continuous tracking along multiple cameras and during abnormal behaviors.

The key challenge for stereo vision is cost, since the counting solution requires special devices and cannot use standard cameras. However, the advantages of accuracy and enhanced metrics make stereo vision the preferred choice for working with the more complicated behaviors.

Video Analytics Platforms

Video Analytics applications running on in-store servers pull streaming videos from all connected cameras and translate the captured video into actionable metrics. The primary advantage is cost—since retailers can use available cameras and also low cost cameras. Another important benefit is the ease of adding data from other technologies such as RFID (radio frequency identification) tags that can enhance the quality of the counts, for example identifying employees.

Due to the lower quality of the original video images, the key challenge of the platform technology is accuracy. Also, by trying to achieve multiple functions such as loss prevention and counting, the positioning of the camera may hinder the results.

Video Analytics platforms have improved significantly in the last few years, and we will probably see many more changes as the larger software and security companies enter the market. The balancing act between accuracy of the best-in-breed technology to the costs and management benefits of all-in-one platform is the dominating factor in the next phase of the Video Analytics market.

WIRELESS

Wireless is an emerging people tracking technology, which is used in unstructured movements inside a large area such as the baggage claim area in an airport or for tracking inside a department store. The technology's dependency on active Bluetooth or Wi-Fi features in the customer's device limits wireless counting to a sampling technique.

Bluetooth Technology

Bluetooth is a wireless technology standard for exchanging data over short distances. It deploys short wave radio transmissions to create secure personal area networks. Bluetooth sensors track the transmissions on a "blink rate" of a few seconds, and are accurate in providing information on a specific individual.

Since each Bluetooth device has a unique signature, Bluetooth vendors can identify the customer at every visit. The core advantage of Bluetooth technology is the ability to provide data on the staying time in the store, the walking path inside the store, and visitor frequency, for specific customers.

While Bluetooth is not suitable for door-counting or queue management applications, it is ideal for in-store behavior, merchandising, and marketing research activities in close proximity.

Wi-Fi Technology

Wi-Fi is the technology standard for exchanging data over a Wireless Local Area Network (WLANs). The Wi-Fi sensors monitor radio waves from the shoppers' smart phones and tablets, and can cover a range of up to 100,000 square feet. Since the emissions of each device (such as a smart phone) are unique, the system continuously tracks the customer from entry to exit, and even beyond the store.

Low costs of setup and maintenance, as well as the benefits of detailed data on the behaviors make Wi-Fi a very attractive value proposition. The success of this technology, however, depends on the activation of the Wi-Fi feature in the shopper's smart phone and addressing privacy concerns.

INSIGHTS ON INSTALLATION

In addition to the cost of behavior measurement technologies such as Traffic Sensors and Analytics Applications, the process of installation can significantly increase the total price of the solution. The more advanced sensors require more time to mount and calibrate. If the solution includes real-time or predictive components, then the calibration requires even more time.

In addition to the cost of mounting the sensors, travel can also play a part if the installation is done in locations far from urban markets, such as North Bay in Canada. This is where the vendor's ability to calibrate the sensor remotely becomes more than a marketing slogan.

Overtime pay is also a consideration since some retailers only allow installation outside the store's activity hours, typically after closing. The costs increase if mounting the sensors requires special equipment for example a lift for ceiling higher than 16 feet, or the cable run from the sensor to the IT room is longer than 100 yards. There are more challenges if the ceiling is hard or the store has designer-oriented architecture. Anyone who has tackled an installation in a store on Rodeo Drive tends to view Beverly Hills California as the road to perdition.

The final piece in calculating cost is on-going maintenance. This includes repairs, replacements, updates and some upgrades that can easily reach 18 percent of the solution, per year.

As Behavior Analytics moves from door-counting to a comprehensive in-store solution, the trend is to combine different technologies. It is not surprising to see a monocular counter at the door, beams inside the store, and stereo video at the frontline area. The key to success in choosing technology is to put the vendor selection process in context to a Customer Service Model.

KEY POINTS

- Capture behavior solutions, which measure customer and employee activities, include beams, thermal, video and wireless technologies.
- Top-down or side beams use infra-red lasers that count when the beam is "broken". Prevalent, simple to install, and low-cost, beams can suffer from inconsistent counting behavior
- Thermal Imaging works by detecting emissions from moving targets, locking on to the targets and then tracking them within the sensor's field of view.
- Video Analytics is the technology to capture an image and analyze its content. The technology is based on identifying and tracking activities, specifically motion detection, line crossing, object recognition, and analytical metrics.
- The balance between accuracy of the best-in-breed technology and the costs and management benefits of an all-in-one platform is the dominating factor in Video Analytics.
- Wireless is an emerging people tracking technology, which is used in unstructured movements inside a large area. The dependency on active Bluetooth or Wi-Fi features in shoppers' devices limits wireless counting to a sampling technique, but provides highly accurate behavior data of individual shoppers.

Chapter 10

SOLUTIONS

Behavior measurement solutions describe the nature of the activities we want to measure, monitor and predict. To be successful the capture technologies require two key components. First, identify the object, whether as people or shopping cart by shape and form. Advanced counters can do more than just capture objects, such as separate the counts of adults versus children by height, and measure as individuals or group behaviors by distance and time. Secondly, translate the activities into measureable data.

Since definitions of behavior measurement solutions (counting technologies) are akin to the Wild West, I took the liberty of defining the behavior measurement solutions based on activity and format. This chapter exists because our industry is being bombarded by new entrants and the marketing jargon is being bamboozled to a point that everyone is getting the idea but hardly anyone agrees on details. We will define behavior measurement solutions by the nature of the behavior.

Activities are categorized by people moving or standing including passing a line; staying within an area; moving from one area to another; and an open or closed zone when no movements are measured. Each of the behavior measurement solutions is categorized by the measured activities, common deployments, and the business objectives they are trying to solve.

PEOPLE COUNTING (PASSING A LINE)

People counting started as door-counting, measuring how many people crossed the main entrance line, in order to calculate the sales conversion from browsers to buyers. Due to the prevalence of technology, retailers should expect that the door counters identify the direction of movement and achieve a 95% or more accuracy rate. Bi-directionality is defined when the system counts a person crossing the virtual line from the outside to the inside of the store as Entry, and when a person passes the virtual line from inside to the outside of the store, the count is considered Exit. People Counting or Traffic Counters are terms referring to motion, the counting of people crossing a line.

Door Counting

Advanced counting sensors introduced important caveats to measuring traffic, such as separating adults and children by filtering the counts by the height of the person. When mother and child enter the store, the child may participate in the buying decision (for better or worse . . .), but from a store perspective this is only a single transaction. By the same token, any variety of group behavior from a family to a customer and employee walking out, side by side, will end up as a single Shopping Unit. The more advanced counters will capture the behavior across the full spectrum of the sensor's field of view and will incorporate the parameters of group behavior while people cross the line.

Door-counting thrives because with traffic, retailers can measure Sales Conversion, a crucial metric for most retailers. For luxury retailers selling discretionary products such as jewelry or electronics, increasing sales conversion by one percent can increase sales by 5 points or more. Some retailers increased their sales by more than 10 points once demand data is available. Even in the destination stores, where people come in with the intent to buy, there are such varieties among stores of the same chain that the retailers can benefit from measuring demand.

Calculated Occupancy

If we know how many people entered and how many people exited, we can calculate how many people are currently in the store. Calculating occupancy of a store, or a closed site, benefits those organizations who deal with limited maximum capacity—such as restaurants or train stations.

Occupancy also plays an important role in countries where over-crowding is the norm. China has strict regulations about occupancy in shopping malls. Anyone who has partied in a popular nightclub in Europe can bless the government insistence on maximum capacity for safety reasons.

Occupancy is also usable in scheduling optimization for Big Box and department stores.

Customer Flow

Customer Flow Solutions indicate where people are congregated in the store, per period of time.

Counting how many people crossed a virtual line has applications beyond the main door. By placing traffic counters in high-traffic pathways, we can calculate changes in customer flow inside the store. Sensors can also create heat maps for real-time analysis of the customer flow.

We can also dissect the store into sections with the traffic counters placed across a virtual line from wall to wall, and measure the flow of people from entrance to the back of the store. This is the poor man's version of measuring the department occupancy, which is good enough for a retailer wanting to test the customer flow in a new concept store or if the store layout works as expected.

In-Store Management (Staying inside an Area)

If People Counting is about crossing a line, than In-Store Management is how many people crossed a line and stayed in an area and for how long. In-Store Management provides metrics on the number of people in a specific area, and their staying time.

Service Management
Service Management is monitoring one person or more standing in the area where they receive service and counting these people as a single transaction. The business objectives are to monitor if there is a customer or not in the service zone, and measure the Service Time.

Technically, the zone is structured as a box and people are measured as long as they are inside the zone. In a service setup, it is irrelevant whether there is one person, two, or more, since the count will automatically be 1.

Service monitoring is useful for time studies such as how long a customer stands in front of a post—office counter, a bank teller, or a customs agent in the airport. Many executives feel that Transaction Time is the same as Service Time, but there are distinct advantages to monitoring the customer side. When the transaction is quick, than monitoring the Service Time, which includes the complete cycle of service with the customer, is more accurate. While real-time feed from the point-of-sale system is a technological nightmare but is necessary for the solutions, such as in Predictive Scheduling, it is easier to monitor the service area. And, in situations where employees tend to slack off, monitoring the customer side is a constructive management tool.

Zone Management
Zone Management counts how many people are staying in a specific area per period of time, and for how long. Contrary to Service Management, in

Zone Management we care a lot about the number of people inside the defined zone and their length of stay. This is why the ability to measure individual staying time is a competitive advantage for technology vendors.

In a Zone, we can define who is considered as staying and who is considered as passing by filtering the staying time. The data cycles into the forecast that a specific activity will translate into sales. For example, did staying more than 10 minutes in a computer display end with a purchase? We can test if the newest digital display is catching interest from customers, if people stop in front of a certain product, or how long shoppers stop at the end of the aisle or at a display counter before checking out, and grab the retailer's choice of impulse goods (ice cream gets me every time . . .).

Department Management
As we discussed in the Browsing Behavior chapter, there are technical and pricing challenges to capture activities in a large area, yet the distinct advantage is the ability to calculate the Department Sales Conversion.

In-Store Behavior Management
In-Store Management combines all the above, as well as Queue Management. We can cover a full store and generate heat maps, or we can pinpoint zones with particular interest. Covering the full store is an expensive proposition and there is only handful of deployments, but newer technologies, especially wireless, promise that in-store behavior is the next big trend in Behavior Analytics.

An important factor of in-store behavior is integration of traffic with point-of-sales for shopping behaviors, with workforce management for real-time deployment, and other applications such as energy management and loss prevention.

QUEUE MANAGEMENT (MOVING WITHIN AN AREA)

Queue Management measures how many people are waiting in line and their waiting time. Another way to view queues is the monitoring of people entering, standing, and exiting an area. The ability of the system to capture both motion and non-motion behaviors, is the technical definition for queue management. If Zone Management measures the motion in and out of an area, Queue Management is about measuring the behavior *inside* the zone.

Moving and Standing

In the chapter Queue Management we discussed the various queue behaviors; therefore here we will point out the core technological requirements for measuring queue length and waiting times. The key point is that while people stand in line, they tend to stop moving. The "standing" may last less than a second or longer than a minute, but if the technology is based on capturing motion it will probably lose the image and stop the count. Some vendors add "computation algorithms" to fix the queue length, but the challenge remains in an accurate capture of waiting time.

Another challenge for capture technologies is when the queue area is longer or bigger than a single sensor. The system must be able to provide a single queue length and continuous waiting time data. This is where many technologies fail, and where costs, quality and experience come into play.

Queue Flow (Exit Speed)

Queue Flow is a special queue solution, where a single sensor measures the exit rate from a queue. The beauty of this solution is that it does not matter how long the queue is, because the only metric measured is how fast the first person in line moves in context to the other waiting customers within the sensor's field of view. This is a complicated behavior which requires expertise in both capture technology and predictive analytics.

This low cost solution is ideal for sites with limited two-three service points, such as a quick service restaurant or a retail bank. Regardless of the open service points, Queue Flow provides information on the Waiting Time.

Queue Snakes (Long Linear Queues)

Queue Snakes are long linear queues, which typically hold more than 50 people at a time. Queue Snakes are also a special case of queue solutions because the number of people waiting and their waiting time in long linear queues can be measured by a combination of Queue Flow and Queue Occupancy—calculated by entry and exit flows—for cost savings.

Queue Snakes are common in the immigration and customs area in airports, amusement parks, conference centers and even in Big Box frontline management.

Frontline Service Management

Frontline Service Management combines data from Queue Management, Door Counting, and Service Management, to answer how many cashiers (stations) should be active for the store to comply with the policies defined in the Customer Service Model.

This solution is ideal for managing bulk cashiers, in formats such as main bank, doubled-deck, or duplex, in a supermarket or a Big Box store. This is also the birthplace of Predictive Scheduling.

Checkout Hubs present different challenges. In a hub format, the checkouts are spread in different places in the store. The large size layout, which requires minimum coverage by employees, limits how much we can optimize the scheduling. It also requires flexible deployment policies and robust alert systems.

Some aspects of the behavior measurement solutions were covered in the theory of Schedule to Demand. We will introduce more deployments in the case studies of Behavior Optimization.

KEY POINTS

- Behavior measurement solutions are defined by the nature of the behavior, including moving or not moving, passing a line, staying within an area, and moving from one area to another.
- People Counting, Traffic Counters, or Door Counting, refer to the measurement of motion, or counting of how many people are crossing a virtual line.
- Service Management is monitoring one person or more, standing in the area where they receive service, and counting the service as a single transaction.
- Zone Management is about counting how many people are staying in a zone and for how long.
- Queue Management is about measuring the behavior *inside* the zone, including both moving and non-moving behaviors.
- Queue Flow is a special queue solution, where a single sensor measures the exit rate from a queue, based on how fast the first person in line moves, in context with the other customers.
- Queue Snakes are also a special case because they can be measured by a combination of Queue Flow and Queue Occupancy—calculated by entry and exit flows—for cost savings.

CHAPTER 11

ACCURACY

Accuracy is the single most important factor in behavior measurement technologies; the definition of accuracy, however, has a far from straight forward answer.

In general, accuracy is a percentage, such as the system counted 95 out of 100 people correctly for an accuracy rate of 95%. The data validation process, however, also requires the consistency and granularity of the data to be considered as accurate. Moreover, auditing of door-counting, queue, and wireless technologies, require different standards because the motion and standing behaviors produce different outcomes.

Another key challenge is identifying the "broken piece" in the audit, which can be either one, or a combination of the technology, technician, auditor, reseller or retail organizations. Since the counting industry does not have generally accepted standards, this is my endeavor at devising our "Best Practices".

THE ACCURACY RATE

Accuracy is the percentage of the system counts to actual behavior. Customer Service Models require at least 95% consistent accuracy for the minimal period of time, such as the 15 minutes for scheduling optimization.

Since there are no acceptable standards, the disputes over the definition of accuracy rage over what should be the sample size, granularity of the sample periods, and the acceptable rate of variance. The accuracy of the metrics depends not only on the ability of a traffic sensor to capture the images correctly, but also the capacity of the system to configure the count solutions to contain and tackle behavior anomalies.

Data Consistency

Data consistency refers to the consistency of the error, over-count or under-count but not both, and avoiding inaccuracy spikes and troughs. To illustrate the consistency principal, we will compare the system's raw output with two video clips. Each video clip runs 15 minutes, for a total of 30 minutes auditing time, and actual count of 100 people entering a store.

If the system counted 100 people and the auditor viewed the video clips and manually counted 100 people entering the store during the 30 minute period, than the correlation is 100%.

If in each of the 15 minute video clips, the system counted 50, and the auditor saw 50 people, then the correlation is 100% for each of the 15 minute periods.

If in the first 15 minutes, however, the system counted 75 people, but the auditor saw only 25, then the correlation is zero. At the same time, in the second clip, the system counted 25, but the auditor saw 75 people in the video clip, then again there is no match. While the 30 minute total counts are the same for system (75+25=100) and audit (25+75=100) for a total of 100 people, inconsistency of the 15 minute counts would have failed the audit.

Blatant examples aside, typical inconsistencies are over-counting and under-counting within the same sample period. In this case, the two errors cancel each other, but two wrongs don't make a right, and this kind of audit should fail.

Queue auditing works on the same concept of consistency. In Figures 11-1 and 11-2, we see an example of auditing consistency errors for queue waiting times.

In an audit of queue wait times made of 12 segments of 15 minute clips each, for a total of three hours, the system's average wait time is 2:81 minutes. The actual average wait time (manually measured from the video clips) was 2: 84 minutes. Comparing the averages, we have an accuracy rate of 99%.

A closer look at the quagmire of details, however, shows disparities. At 4pm the system's average waiting time was higher than the actual time by more than 2 minutes (5:52 versus 3:37 minutes with a variance of 64%). At 5pm, the average waiting time in the system was lower than the actual wait time. (1:13 versus 2:80 minutes with a variance of—60%).

For the 3 hour audit, the system provided 99% accuracy. But, in fact, the audit is a failure, since the system over-counts and under-counts. This brings us to the discussion about granularity—where the sample is only as good as the customer's requirements.

Figure 11-1 Audit Data

Average Waiting Time- 3 Hours audit by
15 Minutes Segments

Period	System	Actual	Variance
15:15	2.16	2.85	-24%
15:30	4.80	5.47	-12%
15:45	3.36	2.49	35%
16:00	5.52	3.37	64%
16:15	3.27	3.17	3%
16:30	1.42	0.98	45%
16:45	1.73	2.67	-35%
17:00	1.13	2.80	-60%
17:15	4.26	3.87	10%
17:30	2.43	2.78	-13%
17:45	1.02	0.61	67%
18:00	2.66	3.09	-14%
Average	2.81	2.84	-1%

Figure 11-2 Queue Auditing - Data Inconsistency

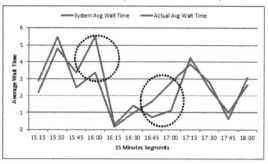

Data Granularity

The sample size and the structure of the audit depend on how the retailer plans to use the data. In the days of scheduling with an excel spreadsheet, most retailers were happy with hourly or daily traffic numbers. Currently, as workforce management systems are full-scale applications with time management, task management and forecasting, many require 15 minute increments of raw traffic data. Only a handful of retailers have a real-time global information system infrastructure, or have deployed predictive scheduling and therefore required immediate updates.

For data granularity, my rule of thumb is 15 minutes for door-counting, 5 minutes for the queuing and service applications, and 2 minutes for the real-time predictive scheduling applications. This is a high bar for most vendors, but this level of accuracy is needed to make the most of traffic data.

Best Practices in Auditing

Auditing, or data validation, refers to a range of processes such as manual audits, real-time audits, and video comparison audits. The objective of the audit is to ensure the system captures the counts correctly and consistently over a period of time. The nature of the audit depends on the solutions, specifically for motion and staying behaviors. For motion, we audit bi-directional counts of people crossing a line, such as people entering and exiting the store. In staying behaviors, we will focus on the more complicated queue management, including auditing queue length and waiting times.

In manual audits, someone manually counts how many people are entering the store or standing in the checkout line, and then these values are compared to what the system produced. While this is the most commonly used methodology; is it also the most prone to error. Just like family stories at the annual holiday get together seem to vary as the years go by and interpretations of the same event can run wild for each family member, manual counting, unfortunately, is not consistent. If there are more than 7 people moving at the same time, the manual count is prone to errors. If the audit time lasts longer than 10 minutes, even experienced auditors tend to miscount.

Real-time audits are another version of manual inspections. Audits are performed when the system is setup with a real-time counting mode, and a technician verifies that the system counted correctly or not, as the people pass within the sensor's path. While real-time audits are better than manual audits, they are still prone to errors. More pernicious methods include changing the system counts in real-time. Nicked named "we-count" it refers to hidden communication between the auditor and the technician interacting with the system in real-time. The person inside the store, with an active, and out of site, mobile phone, counts how many people enter and exit in a loud voice. The person with access to the system hears the counts and if the system's data varies from the actual behavior, changes the raw data of the system in real-time. This way, the actual behavior is changed directly in the system. Bottom line, any audit that includes manual auditing should be avoided.

By far, the best audit methodology compares two system outputs. In video, we compare the system raw files to a manual recount from a video clip. Since both the raw data file and the video clip were generated at the same time, by the same system, the source data is untainted by human bias. Video clips can vary in length (i.e. 5 minutes, 30 minutes). They can be taken during various periods of the day such as 6am or 8pm, which allows for a more complete picture of the traffic counter ability than a one-time audit of 30 minutes in mid-day. We can manually check the video clip multiple times to ensure we are comparing the counts correctly. Moreover, the data validation process can easily be performed by a third-party vendor or by the retailer.

The following audit methods are based on video system-to-system comparisons.

Line Counting

People counting or door-counting is the traditional term for line counting. The audit measures how many people cross the line. Retailers also decide if the audit should adhere to all traffic, or just to one direction. Since this discussion is comparable to the facets of consistency, best practice is to audit per direction.

Time Segments: Traditionally, the counting segment in retail was the hour. For low-traffic stores, a daily rate was sufficient. For Service Intensity, we use 15 minute increments for scheduling and the audit should be done accordingly.

Traffic Level: For statistical purposes, an acceptable level of traffic to determine the accuracy rate of the audit should cover traffic levels of no less than 100 people. Unfortunately, unless the audit is done in a high-traffic store, or we measure only the peak hours, these conditions do not apply. This is why the method of comparing the system's raw data to video clips, in a variety of periods of time and traffic volumes, is best.

Queue Length

Queue audits are more complex than line counting, but they follow the same rules. Queue audits are influenced by the technology and how the system captures images. Some vendors can provide only the averages, maximums and minimums. Some vendors can provide individual tracking and wait time. For queue audits, it is recommended that the retailer fully understands what the vendor considers the parameters of accuracy.

"One in Front" is a common Customer Service Model for Frontline Service Management, for Big Box stores and supermarkets. Common linear queues in retail banking or in quick service restaurants hold, on average, from 1 to 7 waiting customers. Long linear queues (or snake queues) in airports or convention centers can contain more than 100 people at a time. For each solution, the average waiting time determines the required granularity of the audit, while the rules of consistency hold true to all configurations.

For a detailed review of queues, in Figure 11-3 and 11-4, we have a 5 minute audit for a system that tracks individuals, each with their own random identification number (ID) and waiting time. If we only had a summary of a 5 minute segment, with 19 people in the system data (ID 1016 is zero) and in the actual count (ID 1011 is zero) the system error is 0%.

The details provide important insights on the function of the counting system.

Time Threshold: For ID 1016, the system discounted the individual while actually there was a real person standing in the queue for 4 seconds. This event should not be counted as an error because "standing in the queue" requires a threshold and the 4 seconds is not long enough to be considered as a "waiting behavior".

Sophisticated applications can identify and discard events such as an ID 1011 error or an ID 1016 under the threshold, for a more accurate wait time. In our case, we will stick to the simplicity of the average of the 20 recorded events and calculate the variance between the system's average of 1:62 and the actual behavior (manually audited from the video clip) average of 1:78 minutes. The result for the 5 minute audit time is an accuracy rate of 91%.

Figure 11-3 Audit Data by System ID

System Count ID	System Data	Actual (Video Clip)	Count Variance	Time Variance
1001	0.56	0.69	0%	82%
1002	1.73	1.91	0%	90%
1003	3.78	4.23	0%	89%
1004	0.64	0.80	0%	80%
1005	0.38	0.42	0%	90%
1006	0.35	0.41	0%	85%
1007	0.05	0.08	0%	63%
1008	1.92	1.94	0%	99%
1009	2.51	3.75	0%	67%
1010	2.91	3.27	0%	89%
1011	1.05	0.00	100%	0%
1012	0.01	0.05	0%	21%
1013	2.88	3.00	0%	96%
1014	2.93	3.15	0%	93%
1015	0.84	1.00	0%	84%
1016	0.00	0.04	-100%	0%
1017	2.89	3.36	0%	86%
1018	1.92	2.04	0%	94%
1019	0.52	0.55	0%	95%
1020	4.45	4.95	0%	90%
Average	1.62	1.78	95%	91%

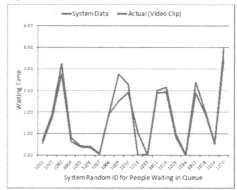

Figure 11-4 Queue Identification Audit - 5 Minutes

"Dropping Error": The system captured images of ID 1010 and ID 1011 incorrectly. The video clip showed an image of 1 person, but the system counted the single individual as two separate people. This is a typical error occurring when a person stands too long without moving and the system "drops" the image from the count.

In our sample database, the threshold for motion/standing behavior is 5 seconds. Since most people stop moving for a couple of seconds when they stand in front of a teller and receive service, audits of Service Time must pay attention to whether the system "let go" of the image and stops the clock when the person stands still. Therefore, the sensitivity and configuration capabilities of the counting system are another facet to consider when selecting a vendor.

If we take out the "threshold" event of ID 1016, we arrive at 18 correct counts out of 19, and a 95% 18/19=95%) accuracy rate. 95% is a superior accuracy rate for a 5 minute queue length. In most situations, 85% to 90% are considered "good enough" accuracy rates.

Waiting Time: Measuring waiting times correctly may be the most challenging component in the people counting market. While the technology improves quickly, correctly capturing waiting time is still on the wish list for most vendors. As a result, the "waiting time" is often a combination of empiric behavior and "corrective" algorithms, and the output is the Average Time or Maximum Time, per period of time.

Group Behavior: Another technical challenge is to capture behavior between two or more people inside the zone. Assume a couple stands in front of the display case, then one leaves the zone for a while and after a couple of minutes returns to the zone, since the virtual area was still occupied, the service time should run through the whole gamut of the sales interaction. Group behavior is hard to achieve technically, and difficult to audit. Proceed with caution.

If the system can generate only Average or Maximum time fields, we can narrow the audit and focus on just one person who leaves the queue with the highest time in a 30 second band. Either way, the parameters of auditing time should be clarified.

Service Time:

The configuration for Service Time refers to how long people stand inside a defined virtual area. While the technical definitions vary between vendors, the business function of service, classifies the occupants of the zone as a single buying transaction (shopping unit). This means that the number of people inside the box can be either zero (none) or 1 (occupied), and as long as the zone is occupied, the system continues to measure staying time.

MANAGING FOR ACCURACY

For the retailer, audits are the holy grail of proving the system's accuracy. Too many times accuracy is the make or break decision for a technology or a vendor. That is a shame since, as we saw, there are many aspects to consider in the decision. Accurate counting requires a technology that captures the images correctly, proper calibration to adapt the traffic sensors to the local environments such as height, zones, and abnormal behaviors, as well as good auditing methodology. Each thread comes from a different company—technology vendor, installation company, Value Added Reseller, and the retailer itself. To prevent mayhem, the retailer's Request for Proposal (RFP) document should ask for and define the auditing requirements.

Some vendors claim the competitive advantage of being both the developer and the marketer. No doubt the close connection between vendor and retailer speeds development and innovation, yet it brings the disadvantage of un-tried (Beta Phase) products and can open the door for mischief. This is where trusting the vendor and a high-quality proof-of-concept process come into play.

Accuracy Statement

Accuracy statements are becoming more common when retailers started demanding the inclusion of an accuracy guarantee into the legal contract. The trick is to read between the lines, and understand the difference between what the technology vendor can do, and what is in the realm of the Value Added Reseller. The bottom line is the higher the accuracy, the more we can trust the data to help us make substantive decisions.

Below is a sample of an accuracy statement by a technology vendor:

The company performed absolute accuracy tests for all device configurations, including counting, queuing, detection, service and tracking. Tests include granularity of audit per individual track and per 15 minute averages; individual and group behavior; adults and children height differentiation; extreme and fluctuating ambient and light environments; customers and staff behavior anomalies; and special parameters; such as shopping carts, for a minimum of consistent accuracy of 98%.

The accuracy of the sensor in use depends on the quality of the installation and on the anomalies of behavior. For maximum accuracy, the company provides auditing parameters and certified training to a third party installer, yet we cannot guarantee the accuracy of the counts seen by the end user. For typical installations, the company expects minimum consistent accuracy levels of 95%.

KEY POINTS

- Accuracy is the percentage of the system counts to actual behavior.
- Customer Service Models require 95% plus consistent accuracy, for the minimal time segment.
- Accuracy of the metrics depends not only on the ability of a traffic sensor to capture the images correctly, but also the capacity of the system to tackle behavior anomalies.
- Data consistency refers to the consistency of the error, over-count or under-count but not both, and avoiding inaccuracy spikes and troughs.
- Data Granularity, the audited time segment, depends on how the retailer plans to use the data.
- Auditing, or data validation, refers to a range of processes such as manual audits, real-time audits, and video comparison audits.
- To prevent mayhem in auditing, accuracy requirements and responsibilities should be spelled out in the retailer's Request for Proposal (RFP).

CHAPTER 12

PLAYBOOK

Successful technology projects work because the objectives, technology and implementation move together in a cohesive unison. The rule of thumb for a winning behavior measurement project is the adaptation of theory to the specific environment of each company. Each retailer has its own identity, and I don't mean as far as category and branding, but in their attitude and ability to work with data. To me, a first sign of failure or success is—does the retailer have the internal framework and senior management support for the project. Armed with the understanding of the Customer Service Model and technology requirements, this chapter is about the process of deploying behavior measurement technologies in the retailer's organization.

Figure 12-1 Behavior Analytics Project Playbook

The playbook has five phases: define the Customer Service Model; select the technology vendors; adapt Schedule to Demand; manage the store in real-time; and optimize the customer experience. Like learning algebra, each phase depends on the previous one, and it is my experience retailers who follow these guidelines, are the ones who benefit the most from Behavior Analytics.

Many traffic projects are initiated by a brave techie in the Information Technology department, or a courageous marketing director, or even by the Chief Executive Officer. Since we are discussing the process of implementing Behavior Analytics in a bricks-and-mortar store, true success hinges on two people—the Vice President of Store Operations and the Project Manager.

If the Vice President of Store Operations does not believe in Behavior Analytics, say thank you and walk away. I can already hear the sales people screaming . . . sadly in my experience, Operations can, and will, sabotage the project if not properly engaged. A more subtle form of failure occurs when the Vice President dictates details. One of the first and most important decisions a retailer makes is to define the leading functional department and then assign the project manager. As a consultant, by far the hardest part of the job is to work with project managers who do not have the empowerment, skills, or feel that the project was "dropped" in their laps. My greatest joy is working side-by-side with smart and motivated people who are open minded and want to learn and make a difference in their company. In our business, we are lucky when the talent is not limited to merchandising, and innovation is a byproduct of a thriving retailer.

DEFINE THE CUSTOMER SERVICE MODEL

Before installing a single piece of hardware or software, retailers should internalize the objectives of Behavior Analytics in the organization. Too many times, retailer executives expect the vendors to come up with an answer, which to me is a self-defeating strategy. The good news is traffic counting has reached the point that most retail managers understand the benefits of measuring demand and sales conversion. Therefore, the process is focused on selecting the best vendor and is handled by the Information Technology department. In-Store Analytics is more complicated, and requires a more substantial internal process to define the Customer Service Model.

We talked at length about Customer Service Models such as "One in Front", "Service Intensity", and "Schedule to Demand" in previous chapters. Therefore, here we will focus on the process.

For every retailer, defining the Customer Service Model should be less about what the competitors are doing, or what the top executives want to achieve, but more about *how* would behavior analytics fit within the culture and infrastructure of the company. How much does the company want to invest in both budget and resources? Retailers should identify the delicate but imperative difference between the necessities of short-term goals and long-term strategy.

Another subtle but important distinction is to understand the dissimilar requirements of corporate and the retail stores. The challenge for the corporate office is to manage the stores remotely and to forecast correctly, but the stores themselves require real-time management tools. Customer Service Models should be attuned to policies set by senior managers and executed by corporate officers, while allowing the stores to accommodate and operate within local conditions. The biggest benefit for Behavior Analytics may be the unmeasured factor, the softer business benefit, which is building the communication bridge between corporate and the stores based on empirical data.

Defining the Customer Service Model process starts with listening. The objective is to translate the different needs and perceptions into a coherent list of objectives and task. This is then prioritized by senior management. When I work for a vendor and a senior retailer executive exclaims "you tell me what to do", I know we are on a rocky road. I tend to get into serious trouble when I am plunged into the middle of a project and see confusion and sense the feel of failure. Taking a breather is a no-no for a vendor, since it breaks the momentum of the sale, yet, sometimes stopping the installation for a while is the more sensible decision in the long run. I love working with sales and technology people but in the end; the priority is what works best for the retailer.

Questions, surveys, and interviews are the tools to define the Customer Service Model. Each function in the business—management, operations, marketing, merchandising, workforce, finance etc.—will use the data for their own specific purposes. It is common for a project to start in one group and later spread the data around the company. By focusing on questions that the policies are suppose to answer, we can start with one functional group and still have the blessing of senior management. At the end of this process we have defined the building blocks of the Customer Service Model and are ready to select the technology and the vendors.

SELECT THE TECHNOLOGY VENDORS

Selecting the technology and selecting a vendor is not necessarily the same thing. While working with more than one company is not ideal, it may be necessary, if the retailer wants to use best-of-breed technology. This is where the behemoth retailers play an important part in pushing for innovation, and, at the same time destabilizing or promoting a startup. The "sandbox process" is probably the best place to test the crucible of disruptive technology.

But if you are not an innovative and budget rich Chief Technology Officer with an appetite for new ideas and competitive advantage, then wait, until the return on investment is spelled out and the technology kinks are cleared, and work with a Value Added Reseller.

Without taking away the importance of internal initiatives and simply liking this salesperson or the vendor, I am a believer in the Request for Proposal (RFP). Aside from the technology requirements, the project includes data management and installation. We have reached a point where the person mounting the sensor in the ceiling does not need to know much about the technology, and the calibration is done remotely by a specialized trained technician. This means retailers typically use their own installation services. We have also reached a point that retailers require an easy-to-use technical interface for managing the system from afar. This is where resellers can add value. This also means the project will likely include at least three different companies. It will also mean that it is very likely that many people in the sales process do not understand what they are selling. Many of these issues can be resolved, or at least minimized, with a properly done Request for Proposal. Unfortunately, most proposals are oriented to the technology and miss out on the implementation needs and business objectives.

Managing the test phase requires different talents and knowledge other than being involved with the roll out to the rest of the chain. The pilot commonly consists of one to four stores and is focused on the technology; in other words—can the vendor execute the requirements of the project. The test phase can vary from 4 to 60 stores, and the focus is on the business objectives and how the retailer will manage, deploy, and scale the project. Typical Proof-Of-Concept (POC) process, from Request for Proposal (RFP) until the roll out purchase order (PO), lasts about 18 months.

ADAPT THE SCHEDULE TO DEMAND

The core of this book provides principles and examples of how to adapt the regular schedule, from a simple change in the beginning of a shift, to the complicated scheduling and forecasts based on the Service Productivity of the employees. Here we will talk about the roles of the Steering Committee and the Working Committee.

The Steering Committee is made up of senior executives, and its nature varies by the type and size of the retailer. The role is simple—define the strategic objectives as well as the budget and execution milestones of the project. The working committee is composed of managers of different functional departments, including operations, workforce, finance, and information technology.

The working Committee typically meets weekly with the vendor and other invited guests, as required. Their goal is to define the details of the framework and be the experts in their relative professions. This is also the phase where the Customer Service Model translates into actionable metrics.

The thorniest challenge is introducing the data inside the organization during the test phase while avoiding the pitfalls that come when people realize that the information impacts their job and how they are used to doing things. This is also the "kill" or "wow" point of the project.

MANAGE THE STORE IN REAL TIME

Return on investment from behavior measurement projects start with better management of the store. After all, one of the Schedule to Demand objectives is to optimize on-site resources deployment to the actual demand. That said, the weak link in a Behavior Analytics project is injecting the tools too early and incorrectly into the store. If the store manager views monitoring activities as "Big Brother" and does not trust the accuracy of the sensors, at worst, the organization develops a resistance to working with traffic counters. Even more injurious to the company, the monies spend on the system are wasted, as data flows without anyone paying attention. In project management, nothing, I repeat nothing, is more important than the process of introducing the solution to stores.

The value of the system to the store is not the same as the value to corporate. Corporate tends to view the retail store in terms of how can I better manage, monitor and plan my business. Store managers care about managing the chaos, monitoring the sales opportunities and operational problems, in real-time, and maximizing their compensation. The return on investment is maximized when the managers' compensation ties their performance to actual demand. Telling managers that they are bound by the sales conversion rate without an understanding of the baseline of behavior, and without building trust in the system is a recipe for disaster.

The key is communication. During the test phase, unless the store managers are especially adroit and are advocates of technology, I don't recommend involving store managers beyond informing them that corporate has, and is, continuously testing the technology. I also recommend avoiding the automatic reports features for at least a month after the data starts flowing. This gives the project manager time to watch the data closely and catch problems. Real-time and predictive applications such as dashboards and mobile alerts should be introduced together with training sessions on the Customer Service Model and the technology. About three months into the testing period, the store managers' inputs are irreplaceable. This is where insights into the challenges of a shift manager will make the real-time user experience invaluable.

OPTIMIZE THE SHOPPING EXPERIENCE

About a year after the data starts to flow, the retailer starts feeling that a transformation is taking place within the organization. The signs are unique to each retailer, but it always happens. The key drops into the hole and the "aha" moment is born. This is a miraculous time, and the one I love the most. This is when retailers embed demand into the fabric of their business philosophy.

Managing the Customer Service Model is about service consistency. If the policy is to "serve 90% of customers in less than 3 minutes", then all stores, across all geography, cultures, and any other characteristics should comply. The idea is that a Dunkin' Donut is a Dunkin' Donut whether the store is a standalone drive-thru in a Houston suburb or in the Atlanta airport. An HSBC bank branch has the same service level, whether in London or Libertyville Illinois. And Tiffany's can test service times from Tokyo to Las Vegas.

Transparency is another important component of service. Customers may not be able to recognize the difference between three minutes or four minutes waiting time, but we can identify changes in their behavior. Displays with average waiting time, for example in airports or amusement parks, seem to enhance comfort, as long as the waiting times do not pass the endurable level.

In short, customers will return to the store if they know that a trip to that supermarket tends to last 10 minutes. Customers will increase their basket if they can find what they are looking for and if not, they feel comfortable asking for help.

Employees create the atmosphere where customers will want to return. Good service will bring a customer back. Great service will make customers tell their friends.

KEY POINTS

- Project Playbook has five phases: define the Customer Service Model; select technology vendors; adapt schedule to demand; manage the store in real-time; and optimize the customer experience
- Defining the Customer Service Model should be less about what the competitors are doing, but rather how Behavior Analytics fits within the culture and infrastructure of the company.
- Requests for Proposals (RFPs) should include technology, implementation, reporting, analytics, and business objectives.
- A Steering Committee role is to define the strategic objectives, and execution milestones.
- A Working committee is composed of managers of different functional departments, and its role is to define the framework of the Customer Service Model.
- Managing to the Customer Service Model is about service consistency, transparency and time studies optimization.

BOOK 3
Behavior Optimization

CHAPTER 13
SPECIALTY RETAIL

So far we have talked about theory and technology, but a counting project succeeds when the traffic data becomes part of the company's fabric and when the metrics of the Customer Service Model are integrated into day-to-day operations. The power of data is in the emotional experience. By far, the best part of working with retailers occurs when a manager suddenly 'clicks', when the data, charts and graphs are translated into a meaningful story, creating a change in perception.

Most people relate retail with buying pants, paint, paper or pearls, hence, retailers who sell distinct goods in the sense they adhere to specific needs, or customer segments, are categorized as Specialty Retailers. In behavior analytics, specialty retail is defined by a distinct dependence on conversion. In other words, in specialty stores increasing the sales conversion has a direct impact on increasing revenue.

The first three months after the data starts to roll-out are the times of discovery. The managers identify the patterns of demand, service and sales conversion, detect missed sales opportunities, and build the Customer Service Model. Below are some case studies from the field. To protect the identity of the customers the details were changed, but the themes remained factual.

THE LUNCH HOUR CROWD

A household goods store described itself as the "treasure hunt for bargains". Customers spend about thirty minutes sorting racks, searching bins, browsing the store in search of plates, pots and bedding. The new, and more expensive, items are displayed in the front of the store, on a wide dais. To keep the fresh look of the store, the manager changed the display every week. The data from the point-of-sale system painted a picture of peak demand in the late afternoon hours, which made sense since the store is located not too far from the train station and the typical customers were people who finished working and were on their way home.

Traffic data showed different demand patterns. Yes, traffic was high on the afternoon, but demand actually peaked during lunch hours. The household goods store was situated in a business center, and there was a rush hour of shoppers around 1pm. A closer look at the transactions showed the lunch hour crowd usually came for the newer items, and while the average baskets were smaller than those in the afternoon, the revenue from each transaction was higher. The surprise of the data, however, was that the sales conversion dropped around 5% in mid-day, practically screaming for attention to the missed opportunities.

The investigation pointed to the frontline checkout process. During the day, the store had four cashiers, plus a shift manager, who also worked at the customer service desk. To accommodate the labor requirements, the two associates who opened the store in the morning, would take their lunch break at 11:30am and be back at work at 12:30pm, just as the checkout line was becoming "very busy".

The drop in sales conversion was attributed to a combination of behaviors. First, because people visited the stores during their lunch hour they had limited amount of time to spend in the store. This means the tolerance for standing in line was diminished. Customers were willing to stand in line for 10 minutes during the afternoon, but tolerance was reduced to no longer than 5 minutes at midday. If more than three people waited in the checkout queue, customers, especially those with one or two items, abandoned their baskets on the floor and left the store.

The schedule, by default, catered to a long line. The logic was to schedule when the people queued up. But it was obvious that having only two active tills while people flowed into the store hindered the shopping experience. The solution was shift changes. The two associates who opened the store would take an early break. By 11:30am there were four active cashiers, just as the lunch crowd started to enter the store. The customers were served quickly and there were no queues in the first hour. This allowed the frontline to serve more customers during the actual peak traffic around 1pm. As a result, the number of transactions during the crowded lunch hours increased by 15%.

Key Point: Scheduling needs to be proactive, not reactive, to demand.

THE DISTRACTION OF DELIVERIES

Located in a busy shopping mall, a high-end apparel store experienced a drop in sales conversion every Tuesday around noon time. It turns out that the store received a delivery of merchandise every Tuesday around 11am. Since it took two hours to unload and sort the goods, the employees were not ready to accommodate the lunch traffic by noon. The delivery time changed to 10am, and sales conversion rose to baseline levels.

Key Point: When a metric behaves inconsistently and out of trend, look closer.

THE ENDLESS DEBATE ON CONVERSION

One of the more insightful debates in behavior analytics relates to the calculations of conversion rates. The question is—should the retailer use the Arrivals or Exiting as the traffic data field. As we saw previously, the answer depends on the objective of the calculation.

A specialty retailer, which emphasizes customer service and where the average staying time in its stores were around 40 minutes, decided to calculate the sales conversion as a percentage of Exiting to Transactions. The rational was that the lengthy staying time distorted the notion of conversion if they would have used the Arrivals field. This way, if 120 people entered and 100 people exited the store during the hour, and the point-of-sales system registered 20 events, than the conversion rate of 20% gives the best picture of the business.

The Key Performance Indicator worked great until the retailer contemplated scheduling policies. As we saw in previous chapters, service intensity (SI) is best calculated by 15 minute increments. The retailer surveyed store managers and customers and the data and decided that the service intensity range should be between 5 to 7. If there were more than seven potential customers to a single sales associate, not only the sales conversion dropped by below 20% but the average basket lost about 5% of revenue. Therefore, corporate mandated that the schedule should adhere to the service intensity range of at least 95% of the time.

The workforce manager happily complied. By scheduling to a service intensity of seven, calculated as the number of people exiting to on-site sales associate, not only could he stay within the limits of corporate policy but also reduce payroll by almost 10 hours per day!

The blame game ignited within twenty four hours. Store managers complained they cannot provide proper customer service "no matter what the numbers say". And corporate wondered if the traffic system counted inaccurately and performed a series of audits. Most importantly, sales dropped, and continued to drop. Long story short, the inquiry pointed that due to the long average staying time the calculation of Service

Intensity with the Exiting data was 5.5, but using the Arrivals metric the Service Intensity averaged 7.1.

Eventually, the retailer found a formula that satisfied all. The daily and periodical sales conversions were calculated as Transactions to Exiting, which for corporate executives allowed a better view of how many people were converted from browsers to buyers. For scheduling and store reports, which used 15 minute increments as the base period of time, the calculations of Sales Conversion and Service Intensity metrics used Arrivals as the data field for demand.

Key Point: The decision how to calculate the sales conversion depends on the nature of customer behavior, staying time and the objective of the calculation.

WHAT'S A STORE MANGER TO DO?

Small specialty stores typically have two to three employees on site, and one is usually the store manager. The standalone stores of a jewelry retailer were not an exception. After reviewing three months of data, the project manager noticed that on occasion, the two associates performed better than three. A more detailed examination brought to light the sales role played by the store manager.

In one store, the manager focused more on sales. In a second store, the store manager emphasized training the new employees. In a third store, two associates worked much better with each other than with the third sales person. This led to a more through process of defining the priorities and responsibilities of the store manager.

As retailers combine more information from traffic and workforce systems, we enhance our ability to better schedule, not only to service intensity, but also to service productivity metrics.

Key Point: To accommodate the schedule to demand policies, one should define the priorities of the store manager, per demand targets.

CAN WE GET AWAY WITH TEMPORARY WORKERS?

Once upon a time there were two retailer chains who decided to increase the number of associates during peak hours. Both retailers sold apparel to teenagers. Both carried the limited help business model on the floor, and the employees ran around most of the time and sorted clothes and shoes.

Each retailer designed a limited pilot to test the concept of adding a single sales person, and the impact on revenue.

While the retailers had no knowledge of the other, the pilots shared many similar characteristics, except one. The West Coast Retailer added a temporary worker and the East Coast Retailer scheduled a seasoned salesperson during those peak hours. The impact of adding the inexperienced associate was limited. For the West Coast Retailer, however, the additional revenue was more than enough to justify the cost of adding a seasoned salesperson.

Key Point: By defining the purpose of the additional salesperson, we gain insight into the type of associate required, and pinpoint the tradeoff between sales and profitability.

SALES VERSUS CUSTOMER SERVICE

Retailers selling wireless phones or electronics have distinct differences between the jobs of sales and customer service. While customer service is an important factor in retention of existing customers, the Key Performance Indicator is "new account growth".

The race for market share has implications for scheduling, since sales and customer service have different training and success factors. At the same time, there is enough similarity between the jobs to move employees around as necessary. Therefore stores have an innate ability to accommodate actual on-the-floor demand, providing that the initial scheduling is done correctly.

One retailer found an innovative solution for the regular schedule by building a ratio of sales versus service personal in order to determine the best possible Service Intensity ratio. A second retailer assigned temporary workers, who could fulfill some of the service responsibilities, the score of half-point. Therefore if the schedule had 3 full-time employees and 1 temporary worker then the Service Intensity calculation used 3.5 as the number of associates. The weighted Service Intensity allowed the corporate managers and the local stores to better communicate the ability of each schedule to adapt to demand.

Key Point: Weighted service intensity is an option when employees serve different functions.

WHEN SPRING STARTS?

It seems we cannot avoid speaking about the weather. In retail, weather plays a significant role, just think boots and plants and cold medicines. In behavior analytics, we seek the correlation between weather and demand. Because weather does funny things to a comparison of store performance, we should take a wider view of the trends, typically with no less than four weeks of data. Since spring in Florida is not necessarily spring in Chicago, our search for data includes where, when, and for how long.

The Storm: When we compare year-over-year results, we should take into account the influences of seasonality and weather. The massive winter storms in the Northeast can last for three weeks, and redefine the shopping habits.

A prominent retailer dealt with measuring the impact of storms by assessing traffic patterns over a period of six weeks. This allowed a respective look at both the downside and the outcome on the business. Traffic data was not modified and the appropriate notations were made in the financial reporting system for future references. It worked because the information technology department is attuned to the needs of the business, and the reporting system allowed for a drill-down insight of the data.

The storm also passed over Canada. Instead of keeping the actual low traffic values for stores in the storm's path, a Canadian retailer decided to modify the traffic data to the previous year's trend. The purpose was to avoid the bias of the storm in reporting traffic for the full chain. Everyone was happy until the following year when a new analyst made assumptions based on the modified data. Chaos ensued. As a result, the retailer moved away from a standalone counting application, and integrated traffic data into a business intelligence application.

The Hurricane: In late August 1992, Hurricane Andrew swept through South Florida. As a Category Five, the massive storm destroyed countless houses and layered cities, causing loss of life and much demand. My most memorable memory was walking into a house with no roof, and walls covered with mud, and broken furniture. The only untouched piece was a China Cabinet with glass figurines, a cherished heirloom of the owners, and a reminder that sometimes we encounter situations with no rational explanation. My second memory is the frantic search for water, gas and power tools.

In the following years, retailers learned to be better prepared, and better stocked, as the hurricanes form in the horn of Africa and move towards our shores. We learned that demand patterns change before, during and after the storm, and while most of the behavior analytics relates to marketing and the buying behaviors, hence the promotions and adjustments of the supply chain, as far as the shopping activities, we can point to an increase in sales conversion. In retail, the distinct behavior of a hurricane is an increase in the intent to buy, people come to buy, not browse, and that manifests itself in the conversion rate.

The intent to buy: An interesting caveat is learning how much the weather impacts demand. For a retailer selling winter coats, this is an important question. Turns out when the weather was colder than average, by up to 5 degrees, the demand and sales conversion went up. On the extremely colder days, the demand decreased as expected, but the sales conversion stayed at the regular level for the store. In other words, assuming all other variables stayed the same, the degree of changes in the weather had a direct impact on the customer's intent to buy.

Key Point: Fluctuations in weather impacts how many people visit the store (demand) and the intent to buy (sales conversion); therefore year-over-year comparison of store performance must take into account the degree and length of the changes in weather.

THE IMPACT OF THE FALL PROMOTIONS

Since the objective of marketing is to bring people into the store, traffic plays a vital role in measuring success. While marketing becomes more personalized, much of the promotions and campaigns are still general in nature. Whether the retailer designs a television ad or a print catalog, we see their impact in the added traffic to the store. If the data is clear, the spikes will tell us not only where was the wave of impact, but when it started, and when it ended. For example, for fall catalogs the typical spike is the week after the campaign starts, and the trend lasts for about three weeks. The challenge is to neutralize the affect of other variables and identify the impact from the promotion.

One way is to connect between demand and other behaviors, such as in-store zone behavior in front of displays, customer surveys, and, of course, the sales conversion. If the demand increases and the sales conversion decreases, we should look at the workforce policies. Part of the story is how early the retailer hired the temporary help for the holidays. If the promotion started in September, and both demand and conversion increased in October, and in November, demand continued to increase but the sale conversion went down, this means hiring had not geared up to demand.

Key Point: To connect marketing to traffic—filter out all the variables but demand. At the same time, define the demand trends in context with scheduling and conversion.

COMPARING HOLIDAYS

In United States, the winter holidays are the most coveted time of the year as shopping becomes a frenzy affair of culture and marketing. Black Friday is a "big deal" in retail, but in our case there is not much that can be done, since the general rule, is all-hands-on-board. A promising area of study refers to how many extra staff members are required, where, when, and in which position.

While some retailers generate about half of their revenue during the season, other holidays serve as an incentive for people to visit the stores. Mother's day is important for luxury retailers, especially jewelers. Easter Sunday is another. Unfortunately, Easter Sunday does not fall at the same date year over year. If the impact of Easter Sunday lasts six weeks, it requires changing the comparison dates. The analysis gets more complicated when Easter Sunday comes during the rains of winter in March, and in the next year during the first heat wave in mid April.

Key Point: Comparing store performance during the holidays requires the year-over-year context of dates, weather and special events.

OPPORTUNITY VERSUS PERFORMANCE

A jewelry chain launched a marketing campaign for Valentine Day based on buy one get one free. The direct result was a confluence of adolescents converging on the store. The tally of the day was simple. From a marketing point of view, demand soared, almost doubling, but sales hardly budged.

A post-mortem of that Saturday showed that the promotion brought in mostly teenagers who bought a smaller than average basket. The stores were not ready for the double scope of visitors. On a typical Sunday the conversion is 15% but on that Saturday, the conversion went down to 12%.

Key Point: Identify the distinct influences of marketing or store operations on sales.

In specialty stores, revenue is a composite of traffic, average basket and conversion rate. If more people visit the store, sales go up. If each customer buys more, sales go up. If a higher percentage of the people browsing the store actually buy, sales go up. Demand results from repeat customers and marketing. Higher basket and sales conversion are influenced by inventory, layout and service. The metrics of behavior analytics—traffic, service intensity, service productivity, staying time, wait time and sales conversion—work best in context to each other. The translation of the raw data into actionable Key Performance Indicators is the objective of the Customer Service Model.

CHAPTER 14
BIG BOX STORES

Big Box stores are, as the name implies, big. The large layout of the store creates a unique challenge for Behavior Analytics. Many Big Box stores serve as an anchor to a mall and are household names, which makes them destination stores. However, the store location influences the customer's intent to buy, for example a mall store serves less as a destination store than a standalone Big Box. In such cases, Sales Conversion plays an important factor. Big Box stores are being transformed as trends of branding first, individual marketing, omni-channels, and store-in-store, together thrust the retailers towards management by analytics.

Big Boxes have a variety of formats. Wal-Mart is a destination store with a bulk, main bank frontline. In Target, sales conversion plays a role. Sears has a checkout hub in each department. Home Depot has three distinct checkout areas, setup as a frontline, but function as hubs, due to the lengthy distance between each section. In Lowe's, the departments are diverse. In Marshal's, the queue is linear. In Burlington Coat Factory customer browsing is a sales model. IKEA is structured as store-in-store. All of those models have a distinct feature—their large and diverse layout, numerous and diversified employees, and a high volume of traffic, make Big Box stores fertile for Schedule to Demand.

WHY HOME DEPOT SHOULD CARE ABOUT TIFFANY'S

Some Big Box stores function as both a destination store and a specialty store. This means visitors typically enter the store with the intent to buy. They browse the store and checkout in the frontline. The identifying mark of these stores is that the business model is to "come, browse, and buy". However, there are specific zones in the store that function as premium service areas. The paint desk in Home Depot is an example. The copy center in Staples is another. In these specialty zones, the associate influences the difference between no sale, average sale, and big sale.

In Home Depot, a Big Box home improvement store, Paint is an important department. Typically stretched across three to five aisles, and manned by three to eight employees, Paint is a churning profit center. The center of the department is the Paint Desk. In the Paint department, customers browse the shelves for products and samples, while employees are tasked with stocking activities. At the Paint Desk, the job is customer service.

The Paint Desk is the hub of activity in the Paint department. Home Depot pays a lot of attention to how long it takes to move a pallet or restock shelves, but has no way to measure the interactions between associates and customers. Since workforce management systems are also attuned to task management, the natural tendency for managers is focus on task completion rather than customer service, even if the Home Depot policy is the "customer first".

In Tiffany's, associates serve customers and every aspect of sales training revolves around service. But in Big Box stores, without measuring interactions between associates and customers, corporate has no way to grade the value of customer service. For example, in peak periods, when the store is packed with people, is it better to keep the associate in a department or redeploy to the frontline? If the store manager keeps the associate in the department, the manager followed the schedule. If the associate serves as a cashier, the store improved the customer's "last touch point".

Big stores tend to schedule by department, but a department is part of a store, and the best way to address real-time bottlenecks and demand fluctuations is by redeploying "floating" associates.

In the same token, Big Box stores also have specialty zones. The zone can be within a department, for example, the Paint Desk in a Paint Department. The zone could also be in a separate area such as the Copy Center in Staples, or the Phone Booth in Costco.

Once upon a time, I went to Michaels to have a picture framed. It was the holiday season and the store had 70% sale on selected frames. I took a couple of pictures with the intent of jumping in and out of the store and spending a bit. I was in the store for three hours, and spend much, much, more. The store has a software program that captures the picture, adds the layout and frame, and creates an image of the end result. Being able to see the picture was an important factor in my decision, but I would have not had such beautiful pictures without help from a former art teacher, an art aficionado, and the person manning the counter, an employee named Marilyn. Such stories abound. Associates do matter, and the more they love their job, the better they are in generating revenues.

As we were working on the pictures, about five people came over, and Marilyn had to call someone for help. My purchase was high because when we started, I was the only customer. None of those other customers bought much. The sale required expertise, attention, and time.

Key Point: Regardless of the nature of the Big Box, departments should be treated as standalone stores, and customer service areas should be managed under the rules of Schedule to Demand.

THE PEACHTREE CONUNDRUM

In the northern suburbs of Atlanta, there is an abundance of streets named Peachtree. From Avenue to Street and Court, the familiarity of the name is confusing, but more important—the streets lead to very different neighborhoods. Some cities are high-income, some not so much. Some are suburbs, some are industrial parks. The dense population is attractive to retailers and it is not unusual to see two stores of the same chain, on the same street, a couple of blocks from each other. These few minutes of driving allow for disparate categories of customers.

The most obvious difference is between home owners and business customers. Home owners shop for themselves. Business customers shop for their companies. Some retailers such as Lowe's or Home Depot home improvement stores have distinct departments, such as garden and hardware. In Costco Warehouse, which sells in bulk, the main target is the business customer. In Kitchen World, home owners are the demand constituency. Big Box stores can address each customer category.

Office supply stores such as Staples or home improvement stores such as Home Depot and Lowe's are great examples for two kinds of customers. A similar conundrum can be found in the behavior of a customer visiting a general merchandise store that also offers supermarket items. Buying milk in a supermarket is a direct result of the intent to buy, hence the destination store. Buying milk in a Wal-Mart or a Target, so far, is an impulse buy and therefore is subject to the analytics of Sales Conversion.

Key Point: The customer's intent to buy, and what, changes the nature of the store, and therefore directly impacts demand trends and sales conversion.

TESTING NEW CONCEPTS

New Concept stores refer to stores where the retailer tests a new business strategy, for example a department store selling food or an office supply store selling electronics. Concept stores also test layout innovation, for example moving flowers next to the main entrance of a supermarket, inserting accessory displays across the main aisle, or even positioning a whole department such as active wear in the front of the store.

Designing layouts is a good avenue for Behavior Analytics. Supermarkets put the milk and eggs at the edges of the stores, in effect forcing customer to go through the less visited aisles in order to get the perishable items. Costco puts booths selling smart phones at the main aisle. Staples situated the computers, phones and printers at the center of the store, pushing the copy center to the back wall. The key to a successful layout is the customer flow, where the high activity sections are forcing people to pass through other areas of interest.

While there are not many full-coverage stores, there is enough data from the field to justify testing at least one new concept store. There are always surprises in customer and employee behaviors, and as we all know, theory and practice do not always coincide.

Key Point: In Behavior Analytics, customer flow is the key to designing new concept stores.

THE STORY OF HELL'S CORNER

Hell's Corner is a store I visited years ago. Hell's Corner was a nickname for the store given to me by a customer waiting in the checkout queue, and it stuck with me as a symbol for severe failure in customer service. While much has happened since, how the store functioned embodies how much a retailer can benefit from the metrics and technology of Schedule to Demand.

Hell's Corner is a story of missed opportunities. Located in the heart of Manhattan, more than 2,500 people visit this Department Store, every single day. The store has three levels—Street Level, Middle Level, and Ground Level—with bulk checkouts, each on the top and bottom floors, and a customer's browsing sales model. While the store regularly lands in the top rank of sales revenue in the chain, it offered one of the worst shopping experiences I have ever seen.

Hell's Corner was a dirty, crowded, dark store, but the highlight of the experience was waiting in line to checkout. The store's location—next to subway and train stations—made it ideal for a customer looking to pick something up on the way to work or on going back home. A quick trip to the store ends up with at least a fifteen minute wait to pay for a bottle of water. The average waiting time during rush hour was more than 30 minutes. Our random survey of the queues produced a 28% abandon rate as customers left the queues, angry, some even muttering obstinacies directed at the checkout staff. Customers showed up because of the store's location and the scarcity of close, similar stores, but it was obvious from talking with the people, the store experienced frequent abandon behavior and most customers avoided returning to the store if another alternative was feasible.

Key Point: High revenue does not necessarily mean the store maximizes the sales opportunity.

Management consisted of a store manager and two shift managers. The store manager's office and the employee area were located in the basement, where the only way in and out was with a rickety elevator that shook in warning sways.

The store manager spend most of his time in his office, on the phone, with no visibility of what was going upstairs on the sales floors. With a look of exhaustion, he explained he does his best to go up and check what is going on, but most of the time the responsibility of managing the frontlines are in the hands of the shift managers. Unfortunately, some managers were experienced and some were not. The chain was not known for training, or paying decent wages. When asked what he wished for, the store manager's answer was quick—"I want to know what is going on in the store, now!"

In many ways, the store functions as two separate stores. The size of the store and the lack of easy access, winding stairways and no escalators, create separate streams of customer traffic, each with its own set of merchandise, frontline checkouts and associates. All the customers I spoke to came to the store with the intent to buy. On the street level, customers desired clothes and household items, and were visiting the store before and after work. Customers on the ground floor were browsing for toys, electronics, books and the typical impulse buys such as soda and crackers. Due to the nature of the trains and subway schedules, the Ground Floor is subject to floods of visitors that easily reach 50 to 100 people at a time.

Street Level Floor

Hell's Corner is located at the gateway of two important streets in Manhattan. Customers trickle in throughout the day, and the traffic peaks in the late afternoon hours. The main entrance is a huge foyer where the visitors take off their coats, pickup shopping carts or baskets, and enter inside by passing between two security gates. The store deploys side beams to count the number of arrivals. During the site survey, a mother kept running after her child, who, despite her efforts, went back and forth between the gates, creating five over-counts instead of none. Later, two women stood so close to the gates they effectively obstructed the beams as more than 10 people walked by. The end tally of the Arrivals data was 80% less than the actual behavior.

Key Point: Due to obvious under-counting and over-counting, and a wide variance between system and actual behaviors, inaccuracy of demand and sales conversion data can lead to irrelevant, and even misleading, conclusions.

In this store, the checkout area consists of three separate queues. The cashier stations close to the entrance gate are used for customer service. For customers entering the store, even two people standing in the customer service queue create the perception of a crowd due to the blocked field-of-view. During peak hours, the front queue can easily reach 10 people.

In the middle of the frontline area is a large wide column. Since the stations are setup in parallel, it forces the store to create two individual queues, one in front of the column, the second in the back of the column. The center queue, in front of the column, and behind the customer service queue, carries about 20 customers in peak hours. Since the entrance to the queue is meshed between the other two queues, the entry point is pushed inside the store to the point where the three front rows of racks are obscured by people. Due to the twisting, customers hold the merchandise in their hands. The center queue does not move fast, and as a result, customers jump in and out of the line. Despite a small sign, the actual entry point to the queue keeps vacillating.

The back queue is a long linear queue, which snakes around stanchions into three rows of lines, with the exit point leading to nine cashier stations. The open area where customers and staff could see each other probably serves as a pressure point to the cashiers to move faster and work more efficiently. During the audit, cashiers in this section performed best as far as Idle Time, Service Time and Queue Wait Time.

Despite being the best performer, the back queue has many flaws. While the exit point has an open field of view, the entry point is half hidden by the center queue. The waiting area is narrow, the turns difficult to navigate with a cart, leading to abandon behaviors. One woman dumped a cart of clothes by the second turn. Two ladies simply gave up and left the full shopping carts in the middle of the aisle. A man with an outsized plastic box on his shoulder kept muttering apologies as he moved around and the box kept hitting other customers. I counted 40 people in an area smaller than space occupied by two cars standing side by side.

Both corporate and managers sensed there was a problem in the layout of the main frontline, and the obvious solution was to rearrange the cashiers along the wall, with a single linear line and one entry and exit point. However, layout design and customer flow were not the only challenges. The shift manager, with over 15 years of experience in the business, admitted the big problem was not the number of employees, but how well they worked. When we audited the Ground Floor, we found that the challenge of managing the cashiers was more serious than we imagined.

Key Point: Parallel queues work in situations where the intent is to encourage customers to stay in the line, such as customers pushing shopping carts, but they also require adequate space.

Ground Floor

In the Ground Floor, the spacious entrance opens up to a huge hall leading to the train and subway platforms. Thousands of people file up the walkway, every day, and a quick dash into the store is an enticing proposition. From the entrance, the wide pathway leads to the depths of the store, and the frontline area is located just off the pathway in the right corner of the store. The queue covers most of the frontline area, but floor-to-ceiling concrete columns and six-feet-high displays surround the checkouts, hiding the labyrinth of the queue. The only portion seen from the aisle is a narrow entry point. The layout, in the form of a long "snake" queue, is based upon the premise, as noted by a staff member, of "let's confuse the customer".

The cashier stations are adjunct to the walls and employees face the queue, in a u-shaped format, with 4 tills to the right, 5 tills on the left, and 5 in the center wall. The queue has five rows, with a tall display case dissecting the customer's field of view between the third and fourth bends. Since the queue's exit point is at the center, the crowded queue and the high display case obscures the field of view from one side to another. In summary, while the cashiers' area is wide open and the queue is linear, the combination of the tall display case in the heart of the queue prevents the shift manager from managing by sight. Effectively, the cashiers are working with no supervision.

The sad part of the story is that the checkout's cacophony is done by intent.

Key Point: "Let's confused the customer" is a policy that encourages bad service *and* over-staffing.

At peak hours, the queue holds 120 people, way outside the frontline area. When customers enter the queue through the official entry point, they see about 30 people in the queue. Little do they know that behind the lofty display case, there are an additional 25 customers waiting. This make the bend around the display case, a key abandon point.

In less than 15 minutes, I saw five customers abandon the queue at that juncture. A memorable abandon behavior was by an elderly man holding bottles of water, who had waited for a at least 10 minutes before reaching the bend and realizing that another 20 minutes of wait time are expected. There was real anger when he threw the bottles into a side display and stormed out of the store.

Key Point: If Abandon Points cannot be avoided, measure and monitor in real-time.

What increased the customers' irritation the most was the behavior of the cashiers. There were 10 active cashiers, but only two girls were efficient and courteous. On one side, a cashier stood in front of the till but instead of serving customers, she was busy texting messages. In the center wall, two cashiers were busy chatting to each other while customers stood in front waiting for the conversation to end. The shift manager was busy at the customer service counter, with no view of the irritant (or irksome) cashiers and no view of the abandon point.

Key Point: To monitor the performance of employees, we can compare the Service Time on the customer side to the Transaction Time from the point-of-sale system.

To be fair, both the store manager and a shift manager had shown the intent to learn and improve, but a proclamation that corporate was not willing to invest beyond a token symbol of improvement and a sense of being overwhelmed, created an atmosphere of ennui and demise in one of the chain's top producers. With Behavior Measurement technologies and the metrics of Schedule to Demand, Hell's Corner could be transformed into manna from heaven.

CHAPTER 15
SHOPPING MALLS

Shopping malls play an important part in generating demand for a store. Traffic data to and inside the mall provides insights into comparing the success of the store in relation to the competitive and economic environment, frameworks of scale and sales cycles, and differences between passing and staying behaviors. This chapter is about measuring the value of a bricks-and-mortar store location.

MY COMPARISONS IN CONTEXT

Traffic data for a shopping mall is good for both the mall operator and the retailer. For a shopping mall, the data provides information on traffic into the mall, per entrance, and per period of time. For retailers, mall traffic helps by comparing the retailer's performance with traffic indexes, evaluating the popularity of the mall, and assessing competitive forces inside the mall.

My Traffic Index in Context

For retailers, a traffic index provides a baseline to compare their performance against the economy and general retail trends. For example, if the country suffers from a recession and consumers slow down on purchases, the retailer can compare its stores to the actual decrease in mall traffic, on a national level. By the same token, retailers can compare the impact of a storm against the region's decrease in foot traffic. With a traffic index, the retailer can isolate the internal performance of the store from the external environment.

Traffic index originated with counting companies who sold counters to shopping malls under the auspices of network hosting and pay-per-data models. It was not only a lucrative business model, but it also provided the counting companies with data from a variety of retailers across a swath of geography, sectors and markets. While traffic companies commit not to divulge the details of traffic and sales conversion, big retailers are moving toward controlling their information technologies in-house—due to unease over privacy and control. While the revenue dynamics changed, most shopping malls stayed on hosting and subscriptions models. The data from these malls serve as the core for traffic indexes.

In North America and Europe, traffic indexes belong to the companies who dominate the counting market in shopping malls. Just like the practice of comparing sales year-over-year (Comp Sales) for the same stores, the traffic index is a composite of traffic fluctuations in shopping malls and some retailers. Simply by using data from one of the largest mall operators, the sample is strong enough to infer national and regional trends in demand.

The good news for retailers is that traffic indexes are sold as a service. You do not have to buy the traffic counters or any behavior solution from the companies. Traffic index is sold independently, as a subscription service, to retailers and news organizations.

Key Point: Traffic index provides a baseline of performance on economy and retail trends.

My Shopping Mall in Context

Retailers open stores in shopping malls with the assumption that the demand starts at the mall. They believe the more popular the mall, the higher the sales opportunity. The decision of where to locate a store, specifically in which shopping mall, is based on location analysis, by zip code, household income, competitors in the area, and other factors. Adding traffic is an important factor in the decision mix.

In one suburb, there were two major shopping malls. They were located at the same crossroads between the major arteries of the city. One was on the north side of the road, and the other on the south. Both malls had the same demographics, same geography, and even some of the same chain stores. Yet today, the South Side shopping mall is flourishing, while the North Side mall is bankrupt. While a host of factors contributed to this story, the North Side experienced a spiral of demand. As fewer people came to the mall, the retailers started to disinvest, leading to less traffic on the upper floor, and then on the main floor, this eventually pushed the better known retailers to leave. The mall was in serious trouble about two years before it closed.

Key Point: Retailers should continuously compare actual demand to the forecasted demand in order for their stores to be functional and profitable.

My Competition in Context

Remember our fictitious Hello and Goodbye stores from previous chapters; the story of Goodbye is based on a real store. Goodbye used to be a successful store until a direct competitor opened a store in a more lucrative location inside the mall, or at least that was the theme held to be true by corporate and store managers. The traffic data changed the perception that the store was not positioned properly, and that a sufficient, and thriving, sales opportunity still existed.

Shopping malls have become more attuned to traffic data. Especially in Europe, shopping malls are measuring traffic per floor, and along the major pathways inside the mall. In a mall in Barcelona, for example, traffic is much higher on the path to an Apple Store than a wireless store on the other side of the stairs. In the same shopping mall, Zara had more traffic than Mango. On the ground floor, the supermarket and home improvement stores face less traffic, but most people entered these anchor stores. The upper floors contained much more traffic, but people hovered in the aisles and sat at the cafes rather than visiting the stores. Location matters. Piggybacking on the mantra of location, location, location, in Behavior Analytics the theme is—traffic, traffic, and, yes, more traffic.

Key Point: Mall traffic data helps formulate the competitive analysis of how my store performs in context with my competition.

DEFINING THE SALES OPPORTUNITY

In a standalone store, the sales opportunity starts when a person actually enters the store. In a mall store, the sales opportunity starts when a person walks by the store. By being in the mall, a person has shown the intent to buy, and, more importantly, we can identify these behaviors. We can measure the opportunity if a person is close enough to the store, if a person stands outside the lease line, but is viewing the display case, and, if we move a sign, does it affect the traffic into the store.

Capturing the Opportunity

Sales Opportunity in a shopping mall starts when a person passes close enough to the store. The ratio between people who pass by and the people who enter the store is considered the Capture Rate or the Opportunity Rate.

Defining the opportunity depends on how far the person must be from the store to be considered a valid prospect. This analysis requires either comparing traffic in the aisle (captured by the mall) to actual number of visitors (captured by the store's traffic counter), or a sophisticated traffic counter (mounted over the store's entrance) that can capture both entry and passing behaviors within the sensor's field of view. While there are differences due to the local layout, we can consider someone who walks within three feet of the store as a valid sales opportunity.

In the chapter on Sales Opportunities, we discussed the challenges related to defining the nature of the visitors who enter the store as a gateway between the mall and the parking lot.

For mall operators, traffic data is a component in negotiating leases with retailers. Comparing mall traffic to the store also offers information on the value of anchor stores such as Macy's or Sears. The data can point to who is pushing the traffic to the mall, the destination store or the shopping mall. If the mall operator tracks customer flow inside the mall, they can provide, or sell, the traffic data to retailers. In Behavior Analytics, therefore, beyond the store, mall traffic data provides an additional level of information on demand.

Key Point: Capture Rate is the ratio of people entering the store to people passing in the aisle.

The Opportunity in Open Stores

Open mall stores offer a unique insight into browsing behaviors and sale cycles. In open mall stores, low display cases are situated along the lease line. Open layouts are widespread for jewelry stores, allowing a better view of the merchandise, even as people are still walking in the pathway. In this case the sales cycle starts outside the lease line, on the mall's side, when the person stops and looks at the display case; this matters, because the door-counters are mounted above the entrance, which means they only measure how many people actually enter the store.

A sophisticated traffic counter can measure how long the customer stood in front of the display and then entered the store (capturing both the motion and standing behaviors). In stores selling luxury goods, the average sales cycle is long and can last 30 or 45 minutes. If there are 3 sales associates on the floor, and one is occupied with a customer for almost an hour, it effectively means the other two sales associates carry the burden of serving all the other potential buyers.

These situations impact the calculations of scheduling, especially if the store experiences this kind of sales in specific periods, such as an increase in wedding preparations, or special holidays. It also helps to understand when the store manager, typically occupied by other duties, should serve as a sales associate. For service oriented retailers, there are many benefits to learn more about the complete sales cycle. This analysis requires an accurate traffic counter, one especially attuned to capturing individual behavior and service times correctly.

Key Point: In open mall stores, the sales cycle starts when people stop in front of the display case, outside the lease line.

Improving the Capture Rate

Stores practice a variety of marketing promotions to entice mall visitors to visit their store, from signs in the walkways to banners and displays.

In one store, located on a corner between two major arteries of shopping, the traffic trends were different per entrance. One entrance faced the food court and the traffic peaks followed the lunch and dinner times. The second entrance opened to the pathway from the main entrance of the mall, and the traffic trends were studied throughout the day.

In another store with two entrances, a tall marketing sign was positioned outside the side entrance, at the walkway. The data showed a 20% drop in traffic from that entrance. Turns out, the sign was moved about 10 inches and literally closed off the entrance. The entry was hidden from the view of people walking down the corridor.

Changes in traffic flows, per entrance, can provide a great topic of conversation with store managers. Once upon a time, I visited an open jewelry store with six display cases situated along the lease line. I casually remarked about the store introducing a new collection to the store, in the second case from the right, about three months ago. I also said the collection was a hit. The store manager was amazed that I knew so much about the store, just from reading traffic data.

Key Point: Traffic data provides pointers on the impact of marketing and displays on demand.

THE JC PENNEY EXPERIMENT (STORE-WITHIN-STORE)

If Hell's Corner is a story of defeat, than the adventures of JC Penny stores are the bold experiment to reinvigorate the department store business model. In Behavior Analytics, the department store functions more as a shopping mall; just as stores are confined and supported by the framework of a mall, the in-store brands are limited and sustained by the department store. This book is not about branding, pricing, or other aspects of store operations except for those factors pertaining to Behavior Analytics, and therefore our concern here is the concept of scale.

Despite their house hold names, Big Box stores are not always pure destination stores. Harrods in London and Macy's flagship in New York are a good example of where many people enter the store for the sake of visiting, rather than buying. In such stores, Sales Conversion plays an important role.

The issue is control. It is obvious that the shopping malls and retail stores are owned by different business entities with complementing and competing agendas. Both entities are served better when more people visit the mall and thus more people visit the stores. The conflict is in the value of the lease contract, and where traffic data adds to an informed decision on both sides. Not obvious and yet similar is the relationship between the department store and the brands. Just think about the latest brouhaha over Martha Stewart's contract with Macy's and JC Penny.

The Store-within-Store concept can be evaluated on the same terms as the relationships between the shopping mall and the retail store. We can measure a Capture Rate based on the ratio of people inside the brand zone to people passing by. We can calculate the brand's Sales Conversion, just as we do in a department area. We can schedule based on demand per brand zone and floater staff members. Basically, we view the concept of the store-within-store similar to two separate entities of a retail store and the shopping mall. Both the department store and the brand owner want more traffic and more sales, the question of who generates the demand, impacts the revenue dynamics.

Scale is the driving force behind this concept. How much does the popularity of the store impact the attractiveness of the brand?—And vice versa. How is the location of my brand's zone impacting the number of people exposed to my brand? This discussion is reminiscent of the endless arguments between Marketing and Operations, which were solved with traffic data. In short, while the concept of store-within-store is new, we can devise the analytics based on the same concepts of monitoring traffic in shopping malls.

Key Point: In Behavior Analytics, we can frame the store-within-store similarly to the relationships between retailers and shopping mall operators.

CHAPTER 16

SUPERMARKETS

Supermarkets are the connoisseurs of data. As pure destination stores, the supermarket's point-of-sale generates massive quantities of data on customer buying behaviors and merchandise trends. Since the stores sell mostly commodity and perishable goods at a low margin, competition is fierce and data paves the path to success.

In Behavior Analytics, the defining solution for a supermarket is Frontline Service Management, the combination of Queue Management and Predictive Scheduling. This is the first of the counting solutions where there is a proven benefit for real-time integration with point-of-sale and workforce systems.

As supermarkets expand beyond the traditional and into retail and services, they face the forces of sales conversion. While the Big Box Stores create a department for food, in essence selling milk and eggs just as they offer bedding and cough drops, supermarkets have had to learn a new way of thinking. From services such as post office, bank and optometrists, to merchandise such as electronics and apparel, supermarkets dabble in the realms of demand and service, the hallmarks of behaviors in specialty retail stores.

Since large baskets lead to shopping carts and bulk frontlines, the checkout stayed as the "last touch point" with the customer. Therefore, the frontline experience should be of a particular interest to supermarkets that compete on customer service.

FRONTLINE SERVICE MANAGEMENT

A Frontline Service Management (FSM) solution measures how many customers entered the store per period of time, monitors in real-time how many people are waiting in line and their waiting time, and predicts how many cashiers should be open in order to prevent the formation of queues.

Frontline Service Management originated in the early 2000s. The company that transformed Queue Management from a wish list into a working technology and business case is Tesco. As the third largest retailer in world, Tesco lives and breathes data. The global supermarket chain has a variety of stores, and therefore frontline formats, from neighborhood stores with a single cashier on site to the behemoths with 70 tills. ASDA (Wal-Mart UK), Morrison's and Kroger followed, and many of the bigger supermarket chains are now testing different varieties of Queue Management.

The return on investment for Frontline Service Management is to reduce the Idle Time and improve Customer Service. Idle Time is measured by the point-of-sale system and is a function of labor costs. The quality of customer service is deemed from mystery shoppers and customer surveys. Managing the checkout experience, however, is optimized with the Customer Service Models such as "One in Front" or "90% of customers wait less than 3 minutes".

Queue Management Solution

We discussed the details of Queue Management and Predictive Scheduling in previous chapters, and how to audit queues in the Accuracy chapter. Here we focus on the point of view of the store.

Counting companies provide stores with a real-time and predictive dashboard, which represents a graphic view of how many stations are active, the average and maximum waiting times, and how many stations should be open in the next 5, 10, 20 minutes.

Some provide a simplified customer display. Some provide mobile applications. Some connect with a point-of-sale system in real-time for transaction data. Some integrate with workforce management systems for a list of on-site employees, their skills and availability.

Network Configuration—There are two core technical configurations for counting solutions. The traditional platform is a traffic sensor, with or without an in-store server, which carries the burden of calculations, and sends only metric data to a central server, typically over-night, in a batch upload. In the last couple of years, some retailers structured their information technology infrastructure "on the cloud", and therefore the sensors send raw data to a central server, where it is processed, and accessed. Business wise, either network configuration works. The impetus behind the decision is the technical versatility by the retailer, costs, and, if appropriate, the impact on accuracy.

In addition to queue data, Predictive Scheduling requires real-time arrivals and transaction data. In closed-loop systems (no real-time connection to point-of-sale), the solution deploys traffic sensors above the service area in front of the cashier to check for present customers, and above the belt to monitor for activity, basket size and scan rate.

Score Cards—In most projects, the managers track performance using a daily score card. Whether the store has 3 or 30 cashiers, the performance metrics are similar. Score cards are calculated daily or weekly, either by the in-store server and uploaded during the night to a central server, or in real-time to a central warehouse.

The objective of score cards is to combine performance metrics from the three operational systems in the frontline—point-of-sale, workforce management, and queue management—for a complete picture of checkout operations.

Queue Management Scores

Whether the Customer Service Model is counts-based or time-based (see Queue Management), the Key Performance Indicators generated by the queue and traffic counting system are—

Queue Service Score—This is the Service Level Measurement (SLM) for the frontline solution. Also known as Queue Measure Score, or Queue Compliance Rate, the Queue Service Score is a percentage of how often the store successfully adhered to the chain's Customer Service Model.

Big Foodie, for example, opens from 6am to 10pm, and there are 56 periods of 15 minute segments used for scheduling. For One in Front policy, the average queue length for each 15 minute segment should be less than 1. If, out of 56 segments in 5 periods the average number of waiting customers was higher than 1, then the Queue Service Score is 91% (51/56=0.91)

Queue Service Scores are typically calculated daily, but retailers also request weekly, monthly, and yearly metrics. Some retailers adhere to a strict service score. Some retailers track the scores but do not impose the success rate on the stores. To preserve consistency, each score should be calculated from the raw data of the original 15 minute segment. Queue data is calculated by the counting system and commonly stored as metrics in the central data warehouse of the retailer.

Average Wait Time—Queue Average Time can be calculated in a variety of ways, therefore it is crucial that the retailer understands how the queue technology works and the underlying process. That said, Average Wait

Time is the simple mean of the average waiting time of the monitored queues, per period of time.

For a system that tracks individuals and their waiting time, the average waiting time is the mean of all waiting times. For example in the auditing sample (see chapter on Accuracy), during a 15 minute period, there were 19 customers waiting and the average waiting time was 1:62 minutes.

Note of caution—Maximum Wait Time is also a common metric. Despite its name, how the queue system works impacts the nature of the maximum time.

Arrival Rate—Demand is measured by the number of people entering the store, per period of time. While traffic is not a crucial metric for destination stores, it is required for Predictive Scheduling.

Measuring the trends of demand is especially useful if the supermarket faces the challenges of sales conversion when entering new venues—such as a coffee shop and electronics. The arrival rate can be 300 people during peak hours and 50 at the closing hour.

Point of Sale Scores
Common performance metrics generated by the point-of-sale system include—

Main Bank Transaction %—The ratio of transactions in main bank to total transactions calculated per period of time. For a daily score card, the data can be uploaded every night to the central server, in a batch process. For example, in a 15 minute period, there were 20 active stations, including main and express lanes. They processed 115 out of 135 transactions for the store, which is 85%.

Self-Scan Transaction %—The ratio of transactions in the self-service stations to total transactions calculated per period of time. We should not confuse the number of transactions by the number of tills. For this metric, it does not matter how many tills exist but how many customers used self-service. For the previous example, 20 out 135 transactions were self-scan, a ratio of 15%.

Scan Rate—The average performance of a checkout operator in the main bank, calculated by the number of items scanned per minute (IPM). For example, cashiers are expected to scan 15 items per minute, or an IPM rate of 15. Scan rate is also calculated per 15 minutes, 30 minutes, or per Hour.

Active Time—Supermarkets count the number of tills signed on by operational hours. For example, if 10 cashiers were active from 6am to 10am, 25 were active from 10am to 2pm, 20 open from 2pm to 6pm, and 15 from 6pm to 10pm, the active time is 280 hours (10*4+25*4+20*4+15*4=280).

Active Time %—The percentage of active time is the Active Time out of Total Capacity Hours; if we have 35 tills, and the store opens from 6am to 10pm, and the active time is 280, then the percentage of active time is 50% (280 active hours / 35 stations * 16 operation hours).

Transaction Time %—Transaction time is measured from the time the cashier starts the event and ends when the cashier finishes the transaction, and includes scan and tender activities. Transaction Time percentage is the ratio of Transaction Time to Active Time, such as 207 hours to 280 hours is calculated as 74% (207/280=74%)

Idle Time %—While Scan Rate measures productivity of the employee, Idle Time reflects the non-operating time of the point-of-sale system. Idle Time includes time between transactions, and the non-active seconds during the transaction.

Idle Time is the Key Performance Indicator of point-of-sale efficiency; for major retailers, shaving one second from the Idle Time saves millions of dollars in labor costs.

Workforce Scheduling Scores

For a Predictive Scheduling solution, the workforce management system feeds how many employees are scheduled for each shift, the names of the employees and skill set. Performance data generated from the workforce management system are—

Forecasted Checkout Hours—The number of "Active Time" hours forecasted for the store. Core advantage of the workforce systems is the ability to create forecasts from the bottom-up, hence from the store, upwards to district, region and finally corporate. For example, Big Foodie has 300 frontline hours for Tuesdays and 500 hours for Saturdays.

Scheduled Checkout Hours—Scheduling employees according to the forecast of "Active Time". Most retailers build the schedule two to four weeks ahead.

Actual Checkout Hours—Actual "Active Hours" used by the store. In our example, Big Foodie had 280 active hours.

Accuracy Scores—The variance between "Active Time" of the forecast, the schedule, and the actual hours. For example, if Big Foodie scheduled 300 and used 280, than the accuracy is 93%.

Both workforce management and queue management solutions predict how many stations should be active. The retailer needs to decide which system takes priority, and how the information should flow between the two systems. While the vendors have yet to sort out these arrangements, the bottom line is a better forecast.

The variance between forecast, schedule and actual payroll hours is a topic of contention between corporate and the store managers It is an endless game between trying to ensure the stores have the right resources and labor cost savings. This is where "soft benefits" such as improved communication are translated into monetary returns.

Proof-of-Concept Challenges

Frontline Service Management requires changes in store operations. In addition to the installation and calibration challenges, the retailer needs to decide how many departments should be involved during the proof-of-concept periods, especially if IT personnel should be involved or not.

The following are common topics for discussion—

Over-Staffing Deployment—If the checkouts are overstaffed, what are the priorities or suggestions for deployment? This may sound simple, but for a high volume store, stocking and re-stocking is an ongoing activity, but so is service in the specialty areas such as deli and meat. Some service zones need skilled employees, some not as many. Again, the question starts with the priority of service and how do we measure the quality of service.

Under-Staffing Deployment—If the system identifies the need to open more stations, the retailer should decide from where to deploy employees. Too many times the answer is to pull cashiers from the service desk. In Big Boxes, retailers tend to move staff from the departments. Part of the process requires time studies, such as how long does it take to close a station in the service desk and open a till in the frontline.

Self-Scan Enticements—A facet of a Frontline Service Management analysis is paying attention to the division between customers checking out in the main bank and those using self-service. Since the number of stations is fixed, the more customers who use self-service the better. As part of the deployment process, the retailer should discuss how to identify such customers, and how to entice these customers to use self-service.

Hybrid Service Model—Optimization is a dynamic process. Since the queue solutions are relatively new, some frontline service solution use hybrid strategies; for example "One in Front" in main bank and "3 minutes Wait Time" in the Express Lanes. The trick is consistency in the Service Level Measurement. Regardless of counting or time-based models, main bank or self scanning cashiers, the goal is to achieve a specific success rate.

The queue solution should also be flexible to accommodate performance values per time of day, such as morning, peak hours, and evening periods. In addition, the system should adapt to the changes in capacity such as broken stations. Finally, the retailer should discuss how often to review the optimal values for each metric, and who should be involved in the process.

Supermarkets with their thirst for technology will find ways to connect to smart badges, mobile scanners, electronic monitors, digital signage, and self-service kiosks to mention a few, to automate many processes. Yet, the technology "Big Data" is not enough. The objective is actionable metrics.

Just like sales conversion is sometimes considered a company trade secret, most supermarkets tend to keep performance metrics close. However, it has been my experience that the hard part is not the value but the process behind the metrics, and there are many benefits to open communication. My point is—do not focus on the value of each metric but on the process of improving Key Performance Indicators and identifying the optimal values for your Customer Service Model.

Key Point: A successful Frontline Service Management project requires robust systems; flexibility to configure sensors, applications and networks to local conditions; management enthusiasm for analytics; and open communication with the stores.

VARIATIONS IN FRONTLINE SOLUTIONS

As supermarkets are actively testing Queue Management solutions, we are encountering slight variations in Frontline Service Management.

Neighborhood Supermarkets—For small stores with 2 to 4 active cashiers and where the average basket is about 15 items, we should assess the queue format. While the parallel frontline is better for customers pushing hefty shopping trolleys, where the baskets are small and the shopping cart can be slim and tall, we recommend the linear queue.

Discount Supermarkets—The use of coupons and discounts at the tills have a direct impact on the length of the transaction, and therefore on the formation of queues. The Customer Service Model and Queue Scores should take into account the longer service time.

No Queue Frontline—When baskets are small and an average transaction is 60 seconds, the stores introduced self-checkouts that carry up to 40% of total transactions. For the few manned cashiers, the result is queue times of less than 30 seconds. These supermarkets "solved" the queue challenge with over-staffing and self-service, and do not perceive themselves as having a "queue problem".

Double Decker Frontline—When there are Front Cashier and Back Cashier, the double capacity exists but is limited by queue length. While retailers can, and do, open both cashiers in peak traffic, the resulting chaos increases the perception of "crowd" and reduces a sense of good service. In the Frontline Solution we can configure an alert when the queue length in the Front Cashier reaches a point where it backend into the Back Cashier.

Duplex Frontline—The Right and Left stations are common in airports, not supermarkets, and yet the frontline solutions share many of the same characteristics. The decision is—should we create two parallel queues, one for each station, or a single queue with a single exit point to both stations. In this case, the layout serves as a factor in optimizing the queue.

Hubs Checkouts—Due to the large distance between the checkout counters, the core challenge with hubs is deployment time. Another facet is minimal requirements for manning each hub. As we discussed in previous chapters, the solution is scheduling "floaters", multi-skilled employees who can assist according to the priorities of deployment specified in the Customer Service Model.

Key Point: Customer Service Models should be adapted to the nature of the Frontline Solution.

Chapter 17
Retail Banking

If I were the CEO of Bank of America, I would hire the Director of Store Operations of Dunkin' Donuts and give him a free hand to analyze, shape, mold, and refocus my retail branches. I am not, nor do I want to be, but I would offer an observation—Quick Service Restaurants and Convenience Stores face the same challenges as a bank branch.

Most bank branches are small, with 2 to 5 tellers sharing responsibilities for counter service inside the bank and services rendered in the drive-thru window, as well as a slate of office activities. The challenge for the bank, therefore, is to optimize the division of limited labor resources among counter service, drive-thru service, and back office activities. If this sounds familiar, it should, because this is also the challenge facing McDonald's, Walgreens, and Starbucks.

In Behavior Analytics, the core solution for such stores, or bank branches, is queue management. This chapter reviews the concept of behavior analytics for a retail branch, the nature of abandon behaviors, and the phenomenon of a single sensor Queue Flow Rate.

The Branch is a Dunkin' Donuts

Retail Banking was the second market, after supermarkets, showing interest in queue management. As is common with counting solutions, Europe, especially Britain, led the way. With an affluent urban population facing congested retail space, retailers searched for innovative solutions. Retail banking is saturated with call forwarding and take-a-ticket technologies, but non-intrusive counting solutions required no participation or activity, such as pushing a button, by either the staff or the customers. Due to the financial storm, the market fizzled for a while, but now it is showing signs of emergence.

Branches work with three categories of customers: those who require teller services, professional services, and the use of the self-service, Automatic Teller Machines (ATM). With time, more simple tasks such as deposits and withdrawals, will be done in the self-service area, or moved online. Due to the lucrative premiums, the bank branches are venturing into professional services such as credit cards, mortgages, and business loans. This left teller services in a conundrum. On the one hand, there is less demand.

162

On the other hand, the tellers are still the primary employees who touch the customer. The trend in retail banking, similar to the bricks-and-mortar retail stores, is to reduce physical sites and compete by promoting customer service.

Behavior Analytics for Retail Banking

A Customer Service Model for the bank branches defines the priorities of the teller services based on actual demand, for counter services, drive-thru services, and task management. Each cashier is assigned to either one of these activities, based on how many customers are waiting for service.

Behavior Analytics is also deployed in flagship and new concept stores to test the layout design, customer flow, in-store marketing, and Schedule to Demand. In context with teller productivity and demand trends, we identify factors influencing the queue length and waiting times.

The Customer Experience—The common customer experience in a bank branch contains two parts, waiting for service, and being served. If, in a retail store, the checkout process is the last "touch point", then in the bank, the checkout is the experience. Since the Stay Time only consists of the Wait Time and Service Time, for a bank competing in customer service, managing the queue is crucial.

Even the basic door-counting solution can provide surprises. We compared two banks. The first was one of the larger branches in the chain, with 8 tellers, 3 self-service stations, and a contingent of professional services. On average, the bank serviced around 3,000 people, per day.

Just down the road was another branch of the same chain. This location was tiny. With the ATM in the vestibule, and 2 teller stations at the entrance, the bank always looked crowded. To everyone's surprise, the smaller bank serviced almost 2,000 people a day, and received higher service scores then the big branch. Turns out the bank employees excelled in moving customers from the crowded ground floor to the spacious and less busy business area in the first floor area. The quick attention to forming queues earned loyal customers.

By any measure of service, the tiny and crowded bank performed better than the big and luxurious branch. The data contradicted perceptions and presented a more balanced and complete picture of what was happening in the banks. This is the driving force of management with Behavior Analytics.

Waiting and Wait Times—For teller services, Queue Management measures and monitors queue length and waiting times, and, if required, can also provide Predictive Scheduling and Queue Flow metrics. We discussed these solutions in previous chapters, and will address Queue Flow later. In comparison to take-a-ticket or call forwarding, queue management is non-intrusive to customers and is not dependent upon actions by the employee. Queue Solutions can be deployed in teller queue areas and professional services waiting zones, which can be combined with the information from the drive-thru data for a complete picture of the waiting experience.

Self-Service Stations—In retail banking, the Automatic Teller Machines (ATM) are an important component of service. Certain banks widened the scope of self-service beyond withdrawals and deposits into more complex transactions such as currency exchanges. Post offices, which function as banks, are less successful with self-service, probably because the quality of customer service is not a high priority for many governments. In Behavior Analytics, monitoring self-service usage, and in some branches measuring the number of waiting and waiting times, is a factor in understanding demand, customer flows, and the customer experience.

Customer Service Model—Once we have queue length and waiting times, we can combine the data with information from the workforce management and point-of-sales systems to build an optimized Customer Service Model, and, monitor the level of service in real-time. The objective is to build the priority between counter service, window service, and office activities. Each branch receives a daily score card with information on Service Level Measurement (SLM) per Key Performance Indicator, for example 90% of customers waited for teller services less than 3 minutes, and 85% of customers waited for professional services less than 5 minutes.

Key Point: In retail banks, the customer experience consists of Service and Waiting components.

Real-Time Behavior Analytics

The Customer Service Model measures the actual demand, how many people are in the bank, how many people are waiting for service, and how many customers are serviced, and formulate, if possible, the recommendations for real-time deployment. The following are common behaviors that impact the formation of queue and service bottlenecks.

Transaction Time—Banks, like retailers, are focused on Transaction Time. They spend resources and company energy on studying activities and procedures with the goal of making the transaction process quicker, and more efficient. While a faster transaction time is to be admired, we should not confuse the efficiency of a better process with the objectives of quality customer service.

Service Time—If the primary user of teller services is the elderly and those who do not speak the local language or have a local account, than the process of customer service, by definition, requires patience, and a longer service time. Our focus here is to formulate a model that accounts not only for the transaction process but also queue behaviors to determine the optimal Service Time.

Complex Transactions—If there are only 2, maximum 3 cashiers, and one cashier is involved with a complex transaction that significantly increases the service time, it effectively renders the cashier as unavailable. This behavior is one of the core factors to formation of queues in non-peak periods. Managers can either assign the transaction to a supervisor or add a cashier, in order to stay within the parameters of consistent waiting times. The alerts are configured for thresholds on a Maximum Service Time, for example a manager is notified when the real-time service time overshoots 5 minutes.

Peak Periods—When the queue is especially long, the objective is to find a way to reduce how many people are in line, such as a supervisor identifying customers waiting only to deposit cash. Branches with no waiting bottlenecks during the week can be overwhelmed when 40 customers enter the bank within a 15 minute period, on a Friday afternoon. A common complaint from bank managers is that corporate scheduling is not attuned to peak demand. In the tally of scheduled to the actual number of employees required to meet customer demand, the mishmash of operations in peak periods wreaks havoc on branch performance.

During the proof-of-concept period we can identify time periods where the transaction level is flat, which is an indication that we reached the maximum capacity of service. Configuration of the alerts can be on either queue length or waiting times, and for rolling periods of 5 up to 15 minutes. Please see the chapter on Predictive Scheduling for alerts configuration.

Abandon behavior merits a section on its own.

Key Point: Spikes in demand, complex transactions, and insufficient flexibility in the schedule are the core causes for the formations of queues.

Nuances in Behavior Analytics

In Behavior Analytics, Retail Banking is similar to other sectors, although there are differences.

Post Office—Government offices are not known for customer service, or productivity, but some are pushing for improvements, even imposing fines on offices incurring too lengthy waiting times. Post offices, and other government offices such as driver's license or internal revenue offices, practice in the same manner as a retail bank; in the sense the stay time is a composite of service and waiting.

Convenience Store—Due to short browsing periods, quick transactions, and typically a single cashier on site, there is not much we can do to affect the waiting time. The objective of queue monitoring is to identify bottlenecks, encouraging self-service in the short term and designing alternatives—such as having two staff members during peak periods.

There are some subtleties in the convenience store format. 7 Eleven or gas station stores share the core characteristics of quick transactions and single cashiers. Walgreens and CVS evolved beyond pharmacy into retail, and while they are still destination stores, conversion rules play a role.

Quick Service Restaurants—The caveat of queue management here is that the waiting in line is at the beginning of the sales cycle. The customer experience, therefore, works in reverse. Checkout out first, browsing (seating and eating) later. Since the customer has yet to spend time inside the store, the abandon behavior is more sensitive. There is less incentive for the customer to stay.

Companies such as McDonald's, Starbucks, Dunkin' Donuts, and Tim Horton's of Canada are lions of customer service. All are focused on processes and transaction time, but a few are measuring the waiting time in order to better position their employees. The objective is to help the store keep the same high level of service, regardless of how many customers enter the restaurant.

Key Point: Nuances in Behavior Analytics for comparable markets, include having a waiting time in the beginning of the customer experience, and the impact of sales conversion.

THE ABANDON RATE

The Abandon Rate has become one of the most over-used and misunderstood behavior metrics in retail banking. Since I had a hand in that, I should stand in the corner and put on the hat of shame, instead, the following is an attempt to set the record straight.

Abandon the Queue

From a technology point of view, capturing abandon behavior simply means identifying a person moving in the wrong direction. If the queue is linear (first in, first out format), we can expect that a normal behavior is to enter the queue from the entry point and leave through the exit point (front of the queue). If the person entered the queue from the back of the queue, stood in line long enough to be counted by the system, and left the queue area by any point other than the exit, this behavior will be considered, and counted, as Abandon.

However, leaving the queue does not necessarily mean abandon behavior. In a bank, some people leave the queue because they are going to the Automatic Teller Machine (ATM). In the post office, customers often leave the queue to fill out a form. Therefore, Abandon counts do not always give a good picture of abandon behaviors.

Audits and customer surveys point out that abandon behaviors are much more pronounced *before* entering the queue.

Not Entering the Queue

It has been my experience that the bulk of the abandon behavior comes from customers who walk into the store see the line and walk out. Three types of perceptions attribute to this behavior.

Too Crowded—If customers perceive that they would have to wait too long for service, they tend to not enter the queue. The predominant perception is "too crowded", which is based on the length of the queue. In Europe, the abandon behavior starts when there are more than 7 people in the queue. However, the perception of "crowd" has cultural and demographic influences and should be defined according to actual behavior in a specific country or region. The secret to abandon behaviors is that despite an increase of traffic into the bank, we see a flat number of customers in the line.

Too Slow—When people perceive that the queue is stuck (not moving), they tend not to enter the queue. We see this behavior in reverse. If the queue is considered long but fast moving, customers enter and stay in the queue. This is a typical behavior in larger banks with more than five tellers, on a Friday afternoon, when customers come in to cash their paychecks.

I Cannot See—This abandon behavior is comprised of perceptions based on the customer's field of view. This is an eye opening exercise to many retail managers. Imagine a stunning bank branch with high ceilings and wide arches, with a teller area in the back. Unfortunately, to a customer standing at the entrance, the teller area always seems crowded, even if it is quite empty, because the field of view does not capture the full area and only offers a glimpse into a darken corner. In another bank, the ATM queue cuts off the entrance to the teller section. These abandon behaviors are a function of faulty layout design, which sometimes can be solved quickly and sometime not.

Not Entering the Branch

This abandon behavior is attributed to customers who stand *outside* the entrance to the bank, see the queue and decide not to enter. While we cannot directly measure how many people standing on the street decided not to enter the bank, we can identify this behavior indirectly when the number of arrivals peaks and stays flat for a period of time. For example, if the arrival rate hovers at 25 people for 4 consecutive 15 minute periods, we can assume this abandon behavior is at play.

Again, layout is a factor. Small branches in high-traffic areas have an obvious challenge. The location of the branch entices customers to come in, but the limitations of capacity create a constant sense of "too crowded". Another example is the impact of outside ATMs. If the ATM is located in the a hall or a vestibule, just before the actual entrance to the bank, a line of more than 2 or 3 people will hide the entry to the bank. For a person standing outside and looking in, any ATM line will hide the main foyer from view.

Not Returning to the Store

Abandon behavior that leads to a decision not to return to the store cannot be measured, at least not by traffic data. However this is a common behavior in highly competitive urban areas.

While abandon behavior is not the single factor of dissatisfaction that leads a customer to change banks, customer service is a factor. Since losing a customer has long-term revenue ramifications, retail banks are more attuned to any signs of abandon behavior.

Key Points: Abandon Rate includes 4 behaviors: abandoning the queue, not entering the queue, not entering the store, and not returning to the store.

QUEUE FLOW RATE

Queue Flow Rate is a unique solution of Queue Management and Predictive Scheduling because it measures the exit rate from the queue, regardless of how many service counters are open.

When the in-store service time is less sensitive to demand, it means the associates are adapting quicker to how many customers are actually waiting for service. In other words, the objective is a customer will leave the queue every 15 sections, if there are two or ten or forty people in line.

Queue Flow Solution—Queue Flow Solution is a single sensor solution, which measures individual people in the queue and their waiting time, in context to other people standing in the queue. Queue Flow is the exit speed, in seconds, from the in-store queue.

The Queue Flow Rate, or Service Time, is calculated in real-time, for a specific rolling period such as 5 minutes, and is displayed on a dashboard or mobile application. The capture technology and the predictive application require expertise and accuracy. To be effective, the solution must pass the auditing guidelines described in the chapter on Accuracy.

The Target Rate—Target Rate is the optimal exit rate from the queue, such as 30 seconds. If there is more than one active station, then this time is divided by the number of available cashiers.

If there is one cashier available, then a customer should exit the queue every 30 seconds. If two cashiers are open, then two customers should exit the queue every 30 seconds. If three service stations are active, three customers should leave the queue within the frame of 30 seconds. This means we keep consistency in the Target Rate.

Key Point: Queue Flow Rate is a cost effective solution for measuring, monitoring and predicting the exit rate from the queue.

CHAPTER 18
COUNTING CROWDS

Why count crowds? Many executives assume that since there is not much we can do to manage crowds there is no point monitoring crowd behavior. While the price of a solution covering a large area is a valid argument for not doing much, this can be augmented by combining counting with other applications such as loss-prevention and predictive scheduling. Measuring crowd behavior in real-time can alleviate and sometimes prevent undesired consequences. Behavior Analytics solutions for crowds commonly consist of monitoring long linear queues and calculating occupancy. Such solutions are typically found in transportation hubs such as airports and train stations, and large facilities such as conference centers and amusement parks.

BALANCING SECURITY AND SERVICE

Airports are fun projects because of their complexity and the variety of behavior analytics solutions that are available for the airside and landside areas. From a customer service perspective, the key challenge is a balance between the foremost priorities of security and the competitive advantages of a better passenger service. To make matters more complicated, airports suffer from the endless tension of the two horse carriage, airport operations and government agencies. And yet, airports are one of the most promising frontiers for behavior analytics.

Passport Control

Most airports have long linear queues in the immigration area. Based on a "First Come First Served"' principal, the long queues accommodate the wary passengers waiting to be processed by immigration agents. In the Singapore airport, long parallel queues stretch from the immigration counters deep into the waiting hall. In the Vancouver airport, the waiting is done in convoluted snake queues under the eyes of shimmering digital screens. In the aged terminal of Berlin Germany, the queues are imaginary and the waiting scene is pure chaos. The bigger airports must deal with more than a thousand people waiting at the same time.

Since people react better to a fast moving line, the convoluting "snake" queue format is the most effective long queue solution. The line moves faster because the nature of the maze layout forces motion. The queue also moves faster because the service times are averaged out. Passengers with longer service time are balanced out by those who are quickly served. Hence processing a family with five passports will be averaged together with the single businessperson. In other words, the efficiency of the snake queue stems from the loosening of the correlation between the length of the queue and the service time.

Deploying a full-tracking behavior measurement solution over such a large area tends to be an expensive proposition, first because of scale and second because airports tend to have high ceilings that need special installation. Therefore, there are two optimal solutions, each serving a different business objective.

The current trend is to install a wireless solution, which accurately picks up Wi-Fi or Bluetooth signals from passengers' phones. This solution provides a good enough sample to estimate the average waiting time across the queue, in a relatively low capital cost. The challenge is assessing the value of the sample. There is no way to appraise how many passengers of the total passengers will have their wireless features activated. Therefore, understanding the crowd behavior will be based on statistical assumptions, which may or may not vary by location or period of time. If the airport objective is to measure the average wait time, this solution works well enough.

Another option is deploying video or thermal solutions. In addition to monitoring the waiting time, these solutions enhance service policies and some also function as a security technology. To counter the price objections, we can customize the solution as a mix of occupancy and queue speed technologies. This requires expertise, so please don't try it on your own! The solutions capture the behavior of the queue and can answer how many passengers are waiting, and for how long, per queue segment and period of time.

The interesting part of the project is answering how many immigration stations should be open. If most passengers wait in the large snake queues, the choke points are in the parallel queues in front of each agent. This is a challenge similar to the architecture of Frontline Service Management, which we covered at length in previous chapters where we focused on queue management and predictive scheduling.

The last word on the immigration area pertains to self-service kiosks. In the last couple of years, the government took a cue from retailers and added kiosks for pre-screened passengers. Currently, these projects are in the pilot phases and are deployed only in a handful of airports.

As a frequent traveler, I salute self-service kiosks, and hope to see more innovations from retail. For many of us in the business world, traveling is an integral facet of the job. Any indication that the airports, airlines, and governments are treating travelers less as a nuisance and more as coveted, revenue generating customers is welcomed.

Security Checkpoint

Managing a security checkpoint project is an exercise of patience. The process is an organizational nightmare since airport operations are managing the queue toward the agents responsible for checking the documents, and a government agency is responsible for the agents and the rest of the baggage checking area. This is the ultimate control paradox, which can be managed by an agreed customer service model. While monitoring the queue wait time is an objective by itself, the soft benefits skyrocket when the process of communication is based on hard data.

Atlanta airport, for example, uses a wireless solution. As a frequent traveler to Atlanta, I can testify to the operational competence of the largest airport in the world. I'm always amazed how fast and efficiently the security checkpoint runs, especially how quickly they add agents and open lanes as the queues grow. Considering the layout and peak passenger flow, the airport still manages the 20-30 minute average waiting time objective, and yes, I checked (and almost got arrested for being too curious . . .).

To maximize the business benefits, the ideal deployment is with a video platform that covers both the counting and security objectives. Since people stand close to each other and the queues are not always clearly marked, the accuracy of the measurement is difficult to achieve. People counting, facial recognition and video management have different technological requirements and platforms. The technology is not there yet, but if current trends are any indication, a good enough solution is around the corner.

Baggage Claim Area

How to better manage the baggage claim area? The question seems more relevant to the background operations of loading and unloading bags, and how many and at what length should the baggage belts be, then how many people are waiting for the baggage. Yet, monitoring how crowded is the area next to the belt provides perspectives on customer service.

For example, one question is how long does it take for passengers to arrive at the belt, the 'walking' time between getting out of the airplane and the baggage claim area. Another is behavior around the belt—how crowded is "crowded", and what can be done to better manage and alleviate the process.

This is also an ideal platform for video since the behavior analytics can be used for both counting and security applications. One of the more interesting areas of research and development is how detailed the system can get to identify certain behaviors. Airports are a natural breeding ground for innovations in behavior analytics.

Retail Areas
Some airports have designated retail areas that function as a de-facto shopping mall, which we have covered in previous chapters. Many airports have situated their retail stores along the long corridors of the terminals, and people traffic can be measured as part of an overall monitoring system. The key objectives are to monitoring the retail area function as they do in a shopping mall, which is to measure per period of time the number of potential customers, and use traffic data as a bargaining chip in lease negotiation.

Airline Check-In
Airlines are probably the only one organization in the airport's hierarchies focused on customer service as first priority. In the check-in area, the typical solution is queue management. Since most situations require a single sensor, this is a relatively low cost solution. It is a worthwhile investment since the details of the number of people waiting and their waiting time, the number of self-service kiosks, and the number of agents on site can help management optimize the check-in experience.

Key Point:
In complex projects of monitoring large crowds in government facilities, the core objectives are to identify management paradoxes and find the balance between security and service requirements.

WHEN MAXIMUM OCCUPANCY IS NOT A JOKE

How many times have you entered a location, a restaurant, nightclub, even a government building, and seen a small sign displaying the maximum allowed occupancy, and wondered does anyone care or pay attention. Well, I do (what can I say . . .). I often feel that occupancy is an ignored number, but over-crowding can lead to dangerous situations and should be prevented.

Years ago, a shopping trip to Hong Kong turned out to be a nightmare. Souks, or open air markets, are an occupancy disaster waiting to happen as people swelter, push and shove, while moving from stall to stall in narrow aisles, but the challenge can also exist in modern shopping malls. A summer day in Hong Kong is an exercise to finding air-conditioning, and a stroll in a high-end department store sounded enticing to me. Unfortunately the idea also occurred to thousands of tourists and shoppers. Luckily, many shopping centers have installed traffic counters and maximum occupancy is enforced by posting guards at the entrances and limiting the number of people entering the store. Measuring occupancy in Asian shopping malls is a big business, and we all benefit from enforcing maximum occupancy policies.

Trains, ferries, and any other vehicles where crowds embark at par with no seat limitations also required close monitoring of maximum occupancy. A movie theater may not assign seats but the number of tickets is limited to the number of seats. When there are no pre-determined limitations for the number of people who can embark, measuring and managing to maximum occupancy is the best way to prevent the safety dangers of over-crowding.

The same logic holds for closed areas such as restaurants and night clubs.

The technological solution, therefore, must do two things well. First, it must be accurate. A solution that is less than 95% consistently accurate will create bias in the numbers. The difference between 210 and 250 people can be the difference between successful or disastrous evacuation during a fire. Two, the system must provide alerts.

Alerts are manifested in a variety of displays such as digital displays for customers, dashboards for in-store staff, and mobile alerts for managers. We discussed the technical context of alerts, including the levels of alerts, frequency, rolling or fixed, and calculations of numbers and percentages, in the Predictive Scheduling chapter. For the solution to be valid, we should first identify the objectives and frame them in the Customer Service Model.

Key Point:
The trick to preventing potential disasters of over-crowding lies in preemptive and enforcement of actions as defined by the Customer Service Model.

THE HARRY POTTER BLUNDER

Our family diligently travels to Orlando every time out-of-the-country guests arrive in the honored tradition of playing in fantasy land, American-style. While Disneyland is the number one destination when small kids are involved, lately Sea World and Universal Studios have become the more preferred destinations. During spring vacation of 2013 we drove to Universal Studio to visit the Harry Potter Exhibit, it had recently opened and was constantly advertised on television.

Our visit started by standing in line for 30 minutes for tickets. Once inside the park, within 10 minutes, we lost a member of our party in the crowd. The area was jammed with people, and we literally stood in the same Hulk Rollercoaster plaza and still did not see our missing person for almost an hour! Hungry, we battled the crowds as we walked toward the coveted Harry Potter exhibit. We were thrilled as we spotted a sign saying "20 minutes wait". Happily we marched forward into the woods only to find later that the sign referred to a waiting line—a second queue before entering the real queue to the exhibit. We spend the next two hours waiting to enter the Harry Potter exhibit.

Inside the narrow, cobbled street of the exhibit, it was hard to breadth as we were surrounded by people. The first rollercoaster showed 150 minutes waiting time. The second line was 180 minutes. We finally found a queue with only 25 people and jumped right in, only to find out the line was for a restaurant. By that point no one wanted to stay. It took another agonizing hour until we were able to leave the park.

Bottom line, we drove for four hours, stood in line for four hours, and drove back for four hours. If our family's response to the late night commercial urging a visit to the Harry Potter exhibit is an indication, Universal Studios has lost its luster . . . Soon enough our adventure has become our favorite tale of a nightmare vacation. Looking back on that day, the good news was—no kids were harmed.

Universal Studios sold "queue buster" express tickets for $100 per person. While this is a brilliant pricing plan, it backfires as a customer service policy. The previous service plan of offering return tickets, per exhibit, would have leveled the traffic flow, and made our time manageable and enjoyable. The additional time would have been probably spent eating and drinking, which could have easily compensated for the cost of the express tickets.

All along in the park, we saw employees manually counting people. What were the numbers? What was done with these numbers? How accurate can they be under the circumstances? To my trained eye, this was not a well-managed situation, and it was obvious some employees agreed. I even heard one blurt that "management does not listen". Sadly, this is a good example how the lack of communication between marketing and operations may lead to short term gain but a much bigger long-term loss.

Customer Service Model is not a fancy theory in an obscure book, but an actionable metrics drive from hard data which serves as a true guide for corporate policy and local activities. These scenarios could have been measured, monitored, predicted, and managed better with a behavior analytics solution.

Key Point
Confusing the customer is not a winning policy to over-crowding, and a bad customer experience tends to backfire. The best solution is to find ways to spread the traffic flow over longer period of time, and if all fails acknowledge and apologies.

CHAPTER 19

TRAFFIC NOVELTIES

Behavior Analytics technologies are improving quickly. The trend points in three key directions. First, the solutions are larger, in the sense that they cover bigger areas such as cities, and are also multi faceted and complex projects such as a full-scale installation in airports. Second, beyond the combination of traffic data with the point-of-sale and workforce systems, the information on people's behaviors is merged with RFID (Radio Frequency Identification) and wireless technologies. These mergers push the market from proprietary solutions to open platforms, which in turn drive the technologies into new arenas. Finally, as retailers developed a taste for people counting, there is demand for analytics technology that can measure more detailed activities. None of these applications has moved beyond the odd pilot and project, but vendors are moving forward, fast.

SCALING PEOPLE TRAFFIC SOLUTIONS

Behavior Analytics can also be applied to very large areas such as cities, stadiums and airports. The application of scale typically interlocks traffic flows with security or energy objectives. This trend is more than just a cost issue; it is about seeing people traffic as a component in a much larger picture of managing operations with technology, in real-time. The counting solutions are, and will continue being, varied by business objectives, companies, and markets; however, the common elements of a behavior measurement solution are the system's ability for central control, real-time monitoring of remote locations, and an analytics platform for diverse behaviors.

Below are recent examples for thermal or video solutions:

Energy Management for Buildings: Smart buildings are energy efficient, and a traffic application helps the system to know when to turn on and turn off the lights. The building can automatically turn off the lights when the area is empty, and turn on the lights when a person walks into the location. One pilot showed almost 5% reduction in energy costs.

Traffic sensors can also be seen in conference rooms. Knowing if the room was used or not, and how many people were in each meeting, improves room scheduling applications.

Video Analytics for Cities: Video cameras in busy pedestrian areas are becoming more prevalent. While the primary application is security and therefore the cameras are not always good enough for more than just storing the video for manual viewing, the trend toward digital and wireless cameras opens the door for video analytics.

Analytics software has yet to catch up with the improvements in hardware, but ability to capture people in motion is a shortcut to finding specific events, quicker.

Customer Flow in Airports: While traffic solutions in airports are sporadic, government agencies, airport management, retailers and airlines around the world are showing keen interest in Behavior Analytics. In addition to the pure security applications, such as facial recognition and remote video monitoring, there is a push toward solutions for improving customer service.

We discussed queue management in immigration control in a previous chapter. Airlines are also interested in counting solutions for their check-in counters and waiting areas. Retailers want to know about the traffic trends in the terminals and retail atriums. Airport operations are paying attention to in-airport train occupancy and the passenger behaviors in the baggage claim lobby.

The complexity of such projects is the multitude of organizations, with different objectives, and where each project has its unique behaviors, all under one roof. It sounds impossible unless we compare it to the task of managing airplanes going up and down all day, within seconds of each other, on one runway. If airports can be, well, airports, there is no good reason why they cannot also be providing quality customer service.

OPEN SOURCE TRAFFIC SOLUTIONS

The people counting industry is a niche no more. As behavior measurement solutions proliferate in retail and other organizations, deployment requirements are pushing the technology away from the proprietary systems into an open platform format. This means data from the traffic sensors can be combined with information from RFID (Radio Frequency Identification) and Wireless technologies.

The applications for customer and employee activities, inside and outside retail, promise countless innovations. The most promising today is the combination of Traffic and RFID which combines data on how people move (traffic) and what they are carrying (RFID). Below are some samples—

Improving Electronic Detection: Electronic Detection Systems (EDS) are notoriously unreliable, and by forcing the system to send alerts only when people walk out of the store (instead of entering or just hanging around the gates), the number of notifications are reduced to a meaningful level, which in turn can be translated into action by employees.

Behavior in the Warehouse: Another application for measuring the relationship between people's behavior and the assets they handle is for moving pallets of goods into and out of the warehouse. We can also measure the stocking activity inside the store. This activity-based-costing is typically calculated manually, but the technology already exists to measure almost any kind of maintenance action that includes a person moving from one location to another.

Monitor the Minutia of Behaviors

The technology for measuring minutia activities, for example a hand movement, is simply not there—yet. As a technology, facial recognition, for example, is easier to develop than people counting. The technology of facial recognition compares a known image (the face of a person we are searching for) to other known images (people in a database or in a video clip). People counting technology must deal with endless variations of people moving and standing behaviors, therefore, in essence, the process of comparison must be dynamic. This is why door-counting, which monitors the straight movement of a person from one place to another, is now more available.

The smaller the details and the more variations of motions we want to measure, the harder it is for the technology to be consistently accurate. That said, technologies tend to leap exponentially once the market demand is obvious, so we should expect much improvement in the next couple of years.

Below are on-going experiments for monitoring detailed activities—

Monitoring for Criminal Activities: The frontline service area is prone to criminal activities, from customers hiding bubble gum and batteries in their pockets, to a cashier who rings the till when no customer is around, the identifying and cataloging of such details are beneficial to loss prevention. The idea of mounting a video camera above the cashier area is not new, but it involves manual viewing to identify wrongdoing. This is one market where there is obvious value for sophisticated behavior analytics.

Monitoring for Hand Washing in Hospitals: Zone Management is used in hospitals, specifically in the operating room, where a traffic sensor is mounted above the hand washing area. The idea is to ensure that employees follow cleaning procedures; therefore if there are five people operating (patient not included), there should be five people entering and exiting the washing zone within a specific period of time.

Now that hospitals are more attuned to preventive measures and check lists, there is much room for introducing behavior measurement technologies.

If there is one thing to take away from the wild success of personal computers, and lately of tablets, it is, even if we do not see clearly the applications, a leap in technology eventually leads to better ways of doing something. In that context, Behavior Analytics is only in the beginning of the journey.

CHAPTER 20
RETURN ON INVESTMENT

Return on Investment (ROI) from traffic projects include direct impacts, such as increase in sales and reduction in labor costs, and indirect returns, such as cost savings from mystery shoppers and the dual-use of video for loss prevention. Each Behavior Analytics solution, people counting, queue management, and in-store analytics, has direct and indirect benefits.

From a cash flow perspective, return on investment is gains minus costs. As retailers wrestle among potential investments and limited resources, the decision should be focused on business objectives. Schedule to Demand serves as a guide for the optimization of store operations and service, and the following is a simplified framework for financial analysis.

ROI for Door Counting

In a door-counting project, the direct return on investment relates to the reduction in labor costs or increase in sales. For most projects, the payback period is six months, with an increase of the sales conversion by 1-2%. Once traffic is embedded in store operations and compensation plans, which for most retailers take three years, the increase in revenue can reach 12%.

Increasing Sales by Increasing Conversion

Schedule to Demand is the process to increase sales conversion in the store. The traditional way is in seeing sales as a function of transactions and the average basket. We can substitute the transaction field with traffic and conversion for the following formula—

Sales = Traffic * Sales Conversion * Average Basket

For a door-counting project, this simple formula illuminates the power of Sales Conversion. Here, the sales field contains the key factors in the store; Traffic refers to demand trends, which relates to branding, marketing and the customers' previous experience with the store; The Average Basket is impacted by inventory and customer service; And Sales Conversion is a Key Performance Indicator for the success of store operations.

Remember our Hello and Goodbye Stores (Figure 20-1). After six months, the Hello Store adapted the regular schedule to traffic trends, and learned to respond to demand in real-time. The result was an increase of conversion rate by 1%. Assuming the average basket stayed the same, daily sales increased by 6%.

Figure 20-1 Increase Sales by Increasing Conversion

	Hello Store		Goodbye Store	
	Baseline	6 Month	Baseline	6 Month
Daily Visitors	1044	1050	1035	1050
Transactions	361	382	276	382
Sales Conversion	35%	36%	27%	36%
Payroll Hours	120	120	90	120
Service Intensity	9	9	12	9
Average Basket	$70	$70	$60	$69
Sales	$25,160	$26,740	$16,560	$26,511
Sales Increase		$1,580		$9,951
Sales Variance		6%		60%

At the same time, the underperforming Goodbye store went through significant changes. The store manager was replaced, payroll increased from 90 hours to the same level as Hello to 120 hours per day, and the average basket rose close to the chain's average with $69. After six months of working with the traffic metrics and adapting the schedule to actual demand, the conversion rate in Goodbye jumped from 27% to 36%. Sales soared 60%.

We can also calculate the estimated annual sales for the chain, using the following formula—

Annual Sales = Avg Traffic * Avg Conversion * Avg Basket * Time Period * Stores

In our 50 store sample, we can calculate the estimated annual increase in revenue (Figure 20-2). We will assume that in Special Chain, the average traffic of 3,875 weekly visitors and the average basket size of $71 stay the same. By increasing the sales conversion by 1%, we see an increase of revenue of 3%. For our Special Chain, the increase in revenue translated into more than $7 million.

Figure 20-2 Increase Sales Conversion by 1%

	1st Year	2nd Year
Average Weekly Visitors	3875	3875
Average Sales Conversion	40%	41%
Average Basket	$71	$71
Number of Weeks	52	52
Number of Stores	50	50
Annual Sales	$286,130,000	$293,283,250

Sales Increase	$7,153,250
Sales Variance	3%

Since Sales Conversion is an easy metric to measure and explain, door-counting has entered mainstream retail. While we offer a wider point of view on why measuring behavior has many benefits, the basic objective of measuring and increasing sales conversion is still the primary drive for any counting solution in a retail store.

Increasing Sales by Targeted Marketing

Another direct benefit of measuring demand is the better management of marketing discounts and promotions. For example, we can target a marketing promotion for a slow period.

Marketing Margin = (Additional Visitors * Avg Basket) - Marketing Costs

For example, if the traffic trend for Hello is 20 visitors between 2pm to 3pm on a Tuesday, and the marketing promotion brings an additional 5 customers, or 25% more demand, and average basket is $70, then the added revenue is $350. If cost of promotion is $75, the marketing margin is $275.

Marketing Margin = (5 Customers * $70 Avg Basket)—($75 Costs) = $275

The calculations for marketing costs can be as narrow as the advertising cost or inclusive with the cost of discount for the products on the sale. These calculations are best handled by a robust pricing application, which can be more attuned to minute changes in demand.

Reducing Labor Costs

Service Intensity drives the process of scheduling. While much of the gain occurs in increasing sales conversion by adapting shifts to traffic, in the service oriented retailers, the tendency is to over-staff, and this is where the reduction in labor costs pay. Over-staffing to avoid bottlenecks and compete with service gained momentum in the last couple of years. The optimization process allows for better positioning and scheduling of employees.

In such cases, retailers can find cost savings by eliminating supervisory duties, adapting beginning and end of shifts to actual traffic, and scheduling employees in context to skills and demand.

Since Schedule to Demand is a relatively new concept, we don't have much data from the field. That said some specialty retailers have seen a reduction of 5 payroll hours per day. Since 4 payroll hours is half a shift, we can make the assumption this is a feasible objective.

To calculate the estimated savings in labor costs we use the formula:

Annual Labor Savings = - Payroll Hours * Hourly Cost * Operating Days * Stores

Therefore, we have a reduction of 4 payroll hours, per day, per store, at an average all-inclusive cost of $15, results in $60 savings, per store, per day.

For the potential annual savings of a 250 store chain, we multiply the $60 daily savings per store by 362 operating days and the number of stores. For our fictitious retail chain, the estimated reduction in labor costs per year is $5,430,000.

Pricing for Traffic Sensors

Most retail stores require a single sensor at the main entrance. Some, due to the width of the door, a low ceiling, or a vestibule, require two sensors. The following price guidelines relate to At-the-Edge traffic counters, Thermal, Single Lens or Stereo Vision Video sensors.

Due to proliferation of traffic companies, prices in the United States and Europe dropped dramatically in last two years. In Figure 20-3 we calculated licensed pricing based on $1,500 per traffic sensor, and the annual support and maintenance costs at 18% from the sensor's price.

Figure 20-3 Door Counting—Retail Pricing

1 Traffic Sensor (with Calibration & Data Validation)	$1,500
Installation (Cabling & Physical Installation)	$250
1 Year Support (18% from sensor's price)	$270
1 Year Cost	**$2,020**
2nd Year Support (18% from sensor's price)	$270
3rd Year Support (18% from sensor's price)	$270
Total Cost of Ownership (TOC) for 3 Years	**$2,560**

There is much variety of quality among traffic counting companies, and retailers should follow the guidelines in the accuracy chapter before making a purchase decision. $2,500 per traffic sensor may be worthwhile, if the store is located on the street and suffers from ambient and temperature challenges to counting accurately.

Retailers should also take into account the details of the support services. The difference in training, help desk, and technical expertise can be the distinction between success and failure. These details should be clarified in the Request for Proposal (RFP) document.

Licensing versus Subscription

The decision whether to license the traffic sensors or using a subscription pricing package has multiple dimensions. While the obvious factor is the price, retailers should put the cost in context to budget and estimate working period.

In the United States, the common subscription pricing for a single traffic counter, reporting and hosting service is about $30 per door. In Figure 20-4, we see a sample of subscription pricing.

Figure 20-4 Door Counting—Subscription Pricing

Installation Fee (Cabling & all labor costs)	$500
Monthly Subscription fee for 1 sensor	$30
1 Year (12 Months) TOC Cost	$860
3 Year (36 Months) TOC Cost	$1,580
5 Year (60 Months) TOC Cost	$2,300

The subscription core advantage is that the upfront fee is relatively low and typically relates only to the expenses of labor, including cabling, physical installation, calibration and data validation. The monthly subscription cost can be taken out of the store's operational budget.

The cons of subscription is that most traffic sensors have 10 working years, which means retailers will pay around double the cost of the sensor for the product life cycle. From a finance perspective, the traffic sensors are assets and therefore are more appropriately placed in an investment budget. Another aspect to consider is that in many cases the retailers lose the ability to determine the type of sensor since subscription, by definition, is a service of traffic data.

ROI FOR QUEUE MANAGEMENT

Queue Management has a direct benefit in reducing frontline labor costs for over-staffed stores, but much of the financial benefits are indirect. We will now address the labor savings and comment on other factors to consider.

Reducing Frontline Labor Cost

In Frontline Service Management, the objective is to open the exact number of stations required to stay within the parameters of the Customer Service Model. Therefore, savings from labor are the variance between the actual number of active cashiers and the target number of cashiers. The calculation is typically done per payroll hour. There is not enough data from the field, but for main banks with an over-staffing policy in Big Box stores, we saw about $1,000 daily savings.

Labor Cost Variance = Active Lanes Variance * Labor Cost per Hour

Going back to Big Foodie Supermarket from Chapter 7, we can calculate the labor savings of opening lanes based on Predictive Scheduling (Figure 20-5). At 6am, Big Foodie would have saved $30 by opening 3 lanes instead of 5 cashiers. For the full day, even with adding cashiers in the midday rush traffic, the store saved $135.

Figure 20-5 Frontline Expense Variance, per Day

Starting Period	Target Lanes	Actual Lanes	Average Queue Length	Expense Variance $15/hour
6:00 AM	3	5	0.4	-$30
7:00 AM	4	5	0.7	-$15
8:00 AM	6	5	1.2	$15
9:00 AM	7	7	0.8	$0
10:00 AM	7	10	0.2	-$45
11:00 AM	10	12	0.6	-$30
12:00 PM	16	15	1.1	$15
1:00 PM	25	20	1.7	$75
2:00 PM	18	20	0.7	-$30
3:00 PM	16	15	1.3	$15
4:00 PM	15	15	1.0	$0
5:00 PM	15	15	1.0	$0
6:00 PM	13	12	1.1	$15
7:00 PM	10	12	0.7	-$30
8:00 PM	8	10	0.8	-$30
9:00 PM	4	5	0.7	-$15
10:00 PM	2	5	0.1	-$45
Cost Savings, per Day				-$135

A side effect of a Frontline Service Management solution is reassessment of the supervisor position, which in turn leads to reduction in duties and therefore payroll hours, and in some cases even the elimination of the job.

Reducing Checkout Idle Time: Idle Time is defined as the number of seconds between transactions or between the periods of time a cashier is not active. It serves as a Key Performance Indicator in high-volume supermarkets. Reducing Idle Time by a couple of percentage points, translates into tens of millions of dollars for large chains. Retailers can measure and monitor transaction times, in seconds, in the point-of-sale system; therefore, reducing Idle Time is an important success criteria for a successful queue management project.

Increase Returned Visits: In using data from the point-of-sale system, retailers have a pretty good idea how often customers visit the store. The correlation between how long people stand in line and returned visits is not direct, but most customer surveys point to waiting time as the number one or two on the scale of quality service.

In a financial analysis, we can conduct a sample customer survey, and assume a certain percentage of added visits relates to improved frontline service management.

Reducing Abandon Behavior: In stores with a business model that emphasizes pricing power and ignores customer service, abandon behaviors is common. Retailers consider their abandon rate as confidential, yet it is not unheard off to hear a10% abandon rate for household name stores. Stories of customer rage, where people ditched their packed carts and left the store, are not rare.

Even a 1% abandon rate can be substantive. If the store lost 10 customers, out of 1,000 daily visitors, and the average basket is $70, the loss is $700 per day. Now assume those customers decided not to return to the store, which means the store loses potential revenue. Take those missed opportunities and multiply by average annual visits and number of stores, and this can run to tens of millions.

Optimizing Carts Inventories: Projects can have a life of their own, and queue management in one store had a surprising insight into shopping cart inventories. Tracking shopping carts improves the Predictive Scheduling but also monitors the actual usage of carts. Better inventory control, equals less costs.

Reduce shrinkage: Positioning video cameras above the service areas benefits not only the queue management but also cashier errors. By combining error alerts from the point-of-sale system with the relevant video timeframe, retailers enhance their loss prevention process. This is an excellent example of dual-use technology.

Pricing for Frontline Service Management
Queue Management takes many forms, from a single sensor to a "snake" long linear queue. In the linear format, pricing for queue sensors follows the same structure as door counting. Frontline Service Management, however, is of a particular interest due to its complexity.

In Figure 20-6, we have a sample cost structure for a main bank in a supermarket with 10 lanes. In addition to the sensor, installation, and support pricing, retailers should take into account the cost of door-counting for predictive solutions, and the cost of dashboards and applications.

Figure 20-6 Queue Management—Retail Pricing

1 Traffic Sensor (with Calibration & Data Validation)	$2,500
Installation (Cabling & Physical Installation)	$250
3 Year Predictive Dashboard ($30 per month)	$360
3 Year Support (18% from sensor's price per 1 Year)	$1,350
1 Sensor Total Cost of Ownership (TOC) for 3 Years	**$4,460**
Number of Sensors (1 per 2 queue lanes)	5
Frontline Service Management 3 Years TOC	**$22,300**
Cost per day, per lane	$6

The pricing challenge for queue management is the cost per store. Covering the frontline requires multiple sensors, and the coverage zone plays an important factor in the pricing calculations. While the pricing may hinder a fast decision, as it should, taken in context to other solutions, the frontline service management solution is an effective technology for retailers where cost management is the norm and customer service is a competitive advantage.

ROI FOR IN-STORE BEHAVIORS

In store traffic monitoring is a nascent market; therefore we do not have a track record for return on investment. But retailers have incentives to try new technologies in order to learn about their customers' behaviors in the store, which allows companies to offer in-store counting technology—specifically wireless and dual-use video analytics.

Increasing Category Sales

Category in this context reflects any specific area we want to measure, whether a department, zone, or a specific category of goods. In the browsing behavior and other chapters we discussed in detail the nuances of measuring and monitoring customers and staff behaviors inside the store. Once we articulate how we measure a behavior, we can monitor progress.

An obvious example is a department sales conversion.

Dept Sales = Dept Traffic * Dept Conversion * Dept Avg Basket

For example back in Yellow Store, we know 100 people visited the Electronics Department, but only 50 visited the computer area. A dedicated in-store promotion for computers can increase traffic to the computer area, and will probably also increase the Sales Conversion.

Therefore we can also calculate impact of the in-store promotion using the formula—

Marketing Margin= (Dept Traffic * Dept Conversion * Dept Avg Basket) - Mkt Costs

The trick is to devise a proper way to measure the area, with consistent parameters, and changing just the single variable for a "before" and "after" comparison.

Reduce Mystery Shoppers Cost: Mystery shoppers are currently the de-facto monitor for in store behaviors, and substituting a "spot check" program with an automatic, always on, system is an attractive proposition to retailers. Same cost, more benefits.

If a cost of one visit is $65, and each store receives 2-3 inspections per month, the annual cost for the store can easily reach $2,000. The costs of the door-counter can be covered just by halving, or more, the number of mystery shopper visits to the store. Again, the more service-oriented retailers, with a robust mystery shopper program, have found in traffic counters a suitable replacement.

Savings from Loss Prevention:
Video Analytics, the technology of measuring behavior with video cameras, is a great example of using the same platform for both loss prevention and sales improvement. While the technology has a way to go before becoming actually dual-use, the trend is unmistakable, and so are the financial benefits. In a return on investment analysis, if the cameras in the store are mounted in positions that are also beneficial for Behavior Analytics, then a percentage of the cost and a percentage of the success in preventing shrinkage should be allocated to the counting project.

ANALYTICS CULTURE!

Perhaps the most important business benefit from traffic data is the unmeasured improvement in the process of managing a store, and the enhanced communication between corporate and the store. The links between traffic and scheduling are so vital that the complaint

I hear most often from store managers is that "corporate does not listen". In my core, I am a financial analyst, but I would venture the analytical competence of the organization, unmeasured but data-based conversations between corporate and the stores, are the most valuable return on investment.

TRENDS IN BEHAVIOR ANALYTICS

Behavior Analytics depends on how retailers combine customer service and demand theories with developments in behavior measurement technologies. In that context, its future is a function of probabilities.

If you would have asked me three years ago where the market would move, my answer would have been focused on the specific applications of counting—sales conversion, queue management and in-store metrics. But a retail company, or any other service organization, exists in the eco-system of technology, business and economics. The influential trends in retail are the mobile connectivity, personalization of marketing, and the competitive advantages of branding. The nature of the bricks-and-mortar store, therefore, must be taken in that perspective.

This leads to two primary trends in Behavior Analytics. First, activities in the physical site must be measured in detail, and monitored in real-time, in order for operations and sales to be optimized. Second, the role of the employee will evolve from a processer of activity to a revenue generator.

Schedule to Demand Rules!

In retail, frontline staff experiences high-turnover and low pay. These are jobs that require little or not much knowledge. The basic assumption is that it does not take a genius to hang the dress on the rack and change prices every two days. This state of mind is starting to change. Specialty retailers, especially sellers of luxury goods such as jewelry and electronics, are aware of the importance of sales training and experience on revenue. Companies such as Starbucks and McDonald's teach basic skills not only to improve customer service, but also to train future executives. Simply put, quality associates require investment and that has a huge impact on how retailers view their employees.

Technology impacts the process in two ways. On one hand, mundane activities can be automated. We see it clearly in self-service kiosks where the customers themselves ping their goods and follow a simple procedure to check out. Many of the supply chain processes are automated. The technology can also invade the in-store realm. For example, creating a digital "dressing room" where customers can try out new outfits, which will not only serve as an enticement to customers, but, as a side effect, will reduce the need to keep putting clothes back on the racks. If the future of the physical store is to also become a fulfillment center, then many of those activities can be done outside the sales floor. The automation of activities, allowing customers to do more themselves and employees to do less, will speed the need to explore the connections between staff, customer and revenue.

On the other hand, we're just starting to explore the connections between the traffic and workforce data. Service Intensity and Service Productivity metrics have yet to cross into retail operations as a core management tool. Moreover, while point-of-sale data provides insights into buying behaviors, the combination of all three data points—traffic, workforce and sales—opens the door for a detailed analysis of the browsing behavior. This has ramifications beyond technology, because transforming associates into knowledge workers not only requires better pay, but also a meaningful environment. The current trend hints that the future of labor in retail is less quantity, more quality.

Video Analytics leads Loss Prevention

Video Analytics is the next frontier in loss prevention. The combination of security and behavior applications is a trend driven more by the technology companies than by the retailers. So far, loss prevention in the store relied on humans watching humans and the pinging of abnormal behaviors such as a cashier returning cash with no customer in the service zone. Video Analytics objective is to automate the process of monitoring abnormal behaviors. This drift occurs simply because video analytics is getting better at identifying individual activities.

Once traffic counters became popular, the behemoth security companies started to explore how to enter the people counting market. The security companies already manufacture, market and install video-based platforms and applications inside the retail store. Adding Behavior Analytics is both a natural progression of the technology and an economic incentive to install cameras throughout the store. While skeptics deride the deployment of multiple uses in the same camera, both technically, and as far as positioning the camera, as costs go down, the know-how improves. The trend points to moving away from "at-the-edge" sensor processing and more towards the "in-store" local network which consists of a server, multiple cameras, and wireless delivery applications.

As technology enters the store with digital displays, facial recognition, wireless tracking and other applications, the ability to define and monitor more detailed activities will transform our ability to analyze the individual behavior. This of course has ramifications on privacy and the challenge of the next decade is finding the balance between business success and individual rights.

Data Driven Bricks-and-Mortar Store

Retail woke up to the benefits of analytics through e-commerce and the competitive advantages of a tightly controlled supply chain. By far, the key challenge in any technology project and deployment is the ability of the organization to absorb the information and work with the data.

From a product life cycle point of view, the traditional traffic counters reached mainstream retail. In other words, most vendors reached the coveted 95% accuracy for door-counters and sensor prices have stabilized. Meanwhile, the more complex waiting (queue) and staying (zone) people behaviors are being defined and packaged and the technology will cross the chasm in the next two or three years. And yet, the technology of behavior measurement has a promising future ahead.

Big Data refers to the analytics of unstructured data. In retail, the challenge is, and will continue to be, sifting through the hordes of raw data—whether from video, thermal or wireless technologies—and translating it into meaningful information. Standalone applications such as the point of sale, supply chain, workforce management and traffic will continue to have specialized requirements, but the desire for simplicity and a "single point of contact" will drive retailers towards compatible platforms and actionable metrics.

Behavior Analytics—The Next Big Thing

Behavior Analytics for retail is an emerging market. Many theories in this book are compiled from a hodgepodge of pilots, partial roll-outs and lots of trial and error. The onslaught of competing and complementing technologies, each with its own pros and cons, constructs a process that is more biased toward a specific desire, rather than a strategic vision for the store. Schedule to Demand aims to change the dynamics by putting the framework first.

The intersections of psychology, marketing, and economic sciences open the door for the induction of Behavior Analytics. If there is a single message permeating this book it is the value of designing the Customer Service Model. Defining strategic objectives, then translating them into policies, and only then choosing technology, makes the process more effective and productive.

Behavior Analytics is the storytelling of customer and employee activities. We sense the wonder in our ability to touch, and smell, and hear, and feel while we shop, and when we don't know what we want, only that we do, an associate can steer us towards that something wonderful that emerges from our desires. The value of the bricks-and-mortar store comes from these elements that make us human, and that is indeed magic.

GLOSSARY

Arrivals Metric counting how many people entered a specific store, per period of time.

Average Service Time Metric measuring the average time each potential customer is being served by a single employee, and is calculated as a period of time multiplied by service intensity.

Behavior Analytics in Retail The science of measuring, monitoring and predicting people behaviors in a retail store.

Bi-Directionality Traffic sensor distinguishing the direction of motion.

Browsing Behaviors Metrics define staying versus passing behaviors in an area.

Checkout Hubs Cashier stations spread in different locations in the store.

Comparable Sales Metric comparing current period sales to the previous period sales, for the same stores.

Customer Flow Counting solution indicates where people are congregated in the store, per period of time.

Customer Service Model Corporate policy of Key Performance Indicators and other metrics for customers and staff behaviors in bricks-and-mortar stores.

Customer Value Ratio of sales to traffic, or the monetary value of an opportunity as defined by a potential customer entering the store and the average sales.

Double-Deck Frontline Checkout format with Front Cashier and Back Cashier stations.

Duplex Frontline Checkout format with Left Station and Right Station.

Exiting Metric counting the number of people leaving the store, per period of time.

Frontline Service Management Behavior measurement solution includes Queue Management and Predictive Scheduling for bulk checkout stations.

Group Behavior Capturing a single shopping unit behavior based on how two or more people relate to each other by Distance and Time

In-Store Demand For a specific area, demand is calculated from Measured Tracking, Measured Occupancy, Calculated Occupancy, or Sampled Opportunities

In-Store Sales Conversion Ratio between transactions and visitors (Opportunity Rate) in a particular area in the store, per period of time.

In-Transaction Behavior Customers move out of the service zone while the cashier continues to scan their shopping goods, and the transaction is still considered in-transaction.

Key Performance Indicators Core metrics measure the performance of a store.

Linear Queue: Linear queues, lines at the entry and the exit are "First In—First Out", and the most common queues.

Main Bank Frontline Cashier stations, or tills, situated one next to each other.

No Queue Customer Service Model where customers checkout immediately, with no wait time.

Occupancy Rate Ratio of traffic in a specific area to total traffic in the store

Occupancy Number of people in the store, in a specific point of time

One in Front Customer Service Model where in any given time, one customer is being served, and one customer waits in the queue.

Opportunity Rate Number of visitors, and hence potential buyers, to a specific area.

Parallel Queues Queue solution monitors multiple linear queues, which run in parallel to each other.

People Counting Technology to count people. Also known as Traffic Counters

Predictive Scheduling Counting solution for real-time redeployment of available labor resources to actual demand.

Project Playbook Behavior Analytics projects have five phases: define the Customer Service Model; select technology vendors; adapt schedule to demand; manage the store in real-time; and optimize the customer experience

Queue Flow Queue Management and Predictive Scheduling solution measures the exit rate from the queue, regardless of how many service counters are open.

Queue Management Counting solution to monitor how many people are standing in line per period of time, and for how long.

Requests for Proposal Document of requirements for technology, implementation, reporting, analytics, and business objectives.

Sales Conversion Measures how many browsers were converted to buyers, per period of time; also known as the Close Rate, Capture Rate, or Conversion Rate.

Sales Opportunities Each visitor to the bricks-and-mortar store represents a sales opportunity; also known as Demand, Traffic, or People Traffic.

Schedule to Demand Method to correlate traffic, sales and labor data, in order to optimize the productivity of store employees and position them where they matter most.

Service Intensity The ratio of customers to employees, per period of time.

Service Level Measurement The percentage of success for metrics in Customer Service Models.

Service Management Monitoring one person or more standing in the area where they receive service and counting these people as a single transaction.

Service Productivity For a given level of traffic and service policy, the probability a salesperson will repeat past sales performance.

Shopping Unit Two or more people acting as a single buying unit.

Staying Time How long shoppers stay in a specific area in the store.

Unstructured Queue A virtual area where people congregated as they wait for service; also known as Cloud Queue.

Weighted Service Intensity Service Intensity Ratio where employees are given different scales based upon their jobs and skills.

Zone Management Measure how many people are staying in a specific area per period of time, and for how long.

www.ingramcontent.com/pod-product-compliance
Lightning Source LLC
Chambersburg PA
CBHW051236050326
40689CB00007B/940